POWERPHRASES! ®

The Perfect Words to Say It Right
and
Get the Results You Want

Meryl Runion

Power Potentials Publishing

SpeakStrong Inc

www.speakstrong.com
www.uniteandconcur.com
www.managementskilltraining.com
www.powerpotentials.com

POWERPHRASES®

Power Potentials Publishing
4265 Outpost Road
Cascade, CO 80809

Runion, Meryl.
    PowerPhrases! : the perfect words to say it right and get the results you want / Meryl Runion ; editor Kristin Porotsky. — 2nd ed.

    p. cm.

    ISBN: 0-9714437-9-3

    1. Business communication. 2. Oral Communication.
I. Porotsky, Kristin. II. Title.

HF5718.R86 2001   658.4'52

QBI01-201211

Table of Contents

Table of Contents continued

NOTE FROM THE EDITOR

It began as a normal editing project, and became a powerful learning experience. When Meryl Runion first told me about her book idea, I thought she was on to something. When she asked me to edit it, I had no idea that I would become indoctrinated into the PowerPhrases phenomenon. Now, everywhere I turn, I see the need for PowerPhrases. Everyone I see needs the communications tools contained in these pages. My family, my friends, my neighbors need them – and I do too. When reading Dr. Seuss to my son I even wanted to teach Power Phrases to Thidwick, the Big-Hearted Moose. I want to edit the sequels.

Kristin Porotsky

Editor
A Second Pair of Eyes
Mother of Four

www.asecondpairofeyes.com

POWERPHRASES®

ACKNOWLEDGEMENTS

My thanks to those who saw the vision that I saw when I decided to write this book. I believed that I had a valuable and useful idea from the very beginning, but the belief of others helped to keep me going.

Thanks to Bill Cowles of SkillPath Publishing. Bill's belief in the idea kept me inspired.

Special thanks to my editor, Kristin Porotsky. With three small children in tow, she took the time to carefully edit and often remembered to tell me that I was "awesome."

I take great inspiration from speaker and author Linda Larsen. Her insistence that this is "not just any book" and that I would have a "huge hit on my hands" gave me more courage than she will ever know.

The encouragement and advice of author Jay Conrad Levinson also provided much needed inspiration from a source that I deeply respect.

I must include my thanks to my dear friend Cindi Myers. After she started reading the manuscript she didn't stop. Her enthusiasm was an inspiration as well.

And of course, I want to thank my family, who allowed me to be married to my book for close to a year.

POWERPHRASES®

DISCLAIMER

This book is designed to provide communications information and guidance. The publisher and the author are not offering legal or other professional services. Every effort has been made to offer advice that is accurate, sound and useful. Results vary in different situations. The author and the publisher cannot be held liable or responsible for any damages caused or allegedly caused directly or indirectly by the information in this book.

If you do not wish to be bound by the above, you may return this book to the publisher for a full refund.

Some boats *DO* need to be rocked. Read more at:
http://www.speakstrong.com/articles/speak-strong/boats.html

PREFACE

The Simple Truth and the Willingness to Tell It:
How PowerPhrases® Were Born

Truth above polls. What a concept. It is quickly becoming a lost art. Truth above polls is about asking yourself what is true and having the courage to let truth, rather than the opinions of others, guide your words.

Summer of 2004, CIA director George Tenet announced he was resigning his post due to personal reasons. It was only after 15 minutes of speculation by commentators about why he resigned that one person suggested…"I think he is resigning for personal reasons." It is a commentary on our times that we are so accustomed to spin we don't even consider the possibility we are being told the truth.

Dishonesty has become so prevalent that we often don't think anything about it. Staff tells management what they think they want to hear without a second thought. We pretend we aren't bothered by something when we are. Performance reviews are whitewashes while managers look for an excuse to pass an under-performer on to another department. All this denial comes at a price. We must be willing and able to hear the truth and to deal with life realistically.

I haven't always had the regard for truth that I do now. I once looked for the convenient answer – the one that would be accepted. I paid an enormous price for doing so.

In 1985, my husband Mike became ill. He was a big, burly guy, and neither one of us thought too much about it. When he didn't get well, I suspected he had cancer. When I mentioned my concerns, Mike became irate. He told me, "Damn it Meryl, I don't have cancer. Don't talk to me about it again. And don't say anything to my mother or anyone else."

The months that followed were excruciating. I watched my husband fade away and was clearly expected to remain silent about my concerns. May 13th, 1986, I lost Mike to untreated cancer.

I did not just lose Mike in that experience. I lost myself as well. I hit rock bottom and was devastated.

Out of the ashes I rebuilt. I was committed to never find myself in a position like that again. My challenge was to find my voice and the words to use it. I had a 32 year habit of deferring to the authority of others. That habit wasn't overcome overnight. It took, and is taking, years of reflection, study and practice to strike a balance. It also took years of trial and error. I went from bottling my responses to blowing-up and attacking. I went through self-doubt about my own motives. Yet, bit-by-bit, I found a balance that has transformed my communication, success level and relationships.

I know my own experience is not unique. Every week in my newsletter, A PowerPhrase a Week, (www.speakstrong.com) I review at least one situation where someone struggles between speaking what is true and speaking what is convenient. I find when people do not have the words to say, they usually say nothing at all. Having the words provides the courage to speak.

I don't want you to have to go through the devastation I did to find your balance. That is why I collect words and phrases that have impact. They'll help you speak when speaking is needed, and they help you speak so people can hear. If you ever had a time when a situation screamed for comment and the words did not come, PowerPhrases will keep you from being tongue-tied again. My audiences love PowerPhrases, and so will you.

I never imagined I would write a book like this one. I was always a "grow from the inside out" kind of person. PowerPhrases grow you from the outside in. Of course, what really matters is simply that you keep growing at all.

Will PowerPhrases work every time, solve all your communication problems and turn your life around? No, no and yes. There will be times when nothing will work. There will be people who cannot be reached. However, the letters I receive weekly reinforce my conviction that a commitment to speaking the simple truth and having the words to do it will, in fact, turn your life around.

INTRODUCTION

A Toolbox of Perfect Expressions

Have you ever needed to express yourself but did not because you could not find the right words? Have you ever walked away from a situation and thought of the perfect thing to say AFTER it was too late? Have you ever given long explanations and wondered—is there a faster, more effective way to communicate?

PowerPhrases! is the answer to these problems and questions. *PowerPhrases!* provides a toolbox of the perfect expressions to get your point across clearly and confidently. This book provides powerful words when you need them the most. You will learn the exact words to use to:

- Assure common understanding.
- Clear up conflict.
- Establish a connection.
- Get what you want.
- Refuse what you don't want.

Knowing what to say results in:

- Increased confidence.
- Enhanced self-esteem.
- Refinement and professionalism.
- The ability to slide out of sticky situations with grace and ease.

While many books tell you what approach to take in addressing challenging situations, *PowerPhrases!* tells you exactly what to say.

> ### Power Pointer
>
> *Few people understand what true power is. True power is not power over anyone or anything. True power is the ability to influence and the ability to get things done. True power in communication is found when the communication gets the results you seek.*
>
> *Take a look at the roots of the word communication. It comes from the word communion. Communication is effective when it builds a bridge between speaker and listener.*
>
> *If you are looking for a book to give you power over others, PowerPhrases! is not it. If you are looking for a book to help you build bridges and dissolve barriers, this is the book for you. Read on to find the tools you are looking for.*

How to Use PowerPhrases!

1. Read through *PowerPhrases!* cover-to-cover at least once to get an overview of what a PowerPhrase is. Then read it again to select the PowerPhrases you like and that are most useful to you. I have highlighted and bulleted the PowerPhrases so you can find them with ease. Memorize them. Put them on your fridge, next to your bed and on your bathroom mirror. Practice them until they become automatic. Better yet, practice using them with a role-play partner. Have someone play a person you need to address while you practice your PowerPhrases. You'll find that the words will come more easily if you have practiced them in a safe environment.

2. Use *PowerPhrases!* as a reference when you prepare to face a challenging situation. Look up the situation and learn the key phrases that make sense to you.

3. Whenever you have a situation that does not go as well as you want, return to the book and pick what you wish you had said. The PowerPhrase will be ready to use the next time.

4. Subscribe to A *PowerPhrase a Week*, a weekly email newsletter, by visiting *www.SpeakStrong.com*. It will develop your use of PowerPhrases one week at a time.

Be Aware Who Speaks When You Open Your Mouth

Have you ever wanted to be nice and nasty at the same time? Have you ever wanted to simultaneously affirm and affront someone? If so, do you wonder why, and perhaps even question your own sanity? You are not alone. There is a story from the Cherokees that helps us understand why this happens.

The Two Wolves

An elder Cherokee Native American was teaching his grandchildren about life. He said to them, "A fight is going on inside me... it is a terrible fight and it is between two wolves.

"One wolf represents fear, anger, envy, sorrow, regret, greed, arrogance, self-pity, guilt, resentment, inferiority, lies, false pride, superiority, and ego.

"The other stands for joy, peace, love, hope, sharing, serenity, humility, kindness, benevolence, friendship, empathy, generosity, truth, compassion, and faith.

"This same fight is going on inside you, and inside every other person, too."

The children thought about it for a minute and then one child asked, "Which wolf will win, Grandfather?"

The old Cherokee simply replied... "The one you feed."

What Do You Feed?

Every single thought you have can feed one wolf or the other. It is important to think about how you think to know which wolf you are feeding.

Rather than talk in terms of wolves, I talk about Izzie the lizard and Pippi the giraffe. Izzie represents the reptilian brain. We all have one. It is the first one to develop and it is responsible for sensory-motor coordination. It is preverbal and controls life functioning. Its impulses are instinctual and ritualistic, and it is concerned with survival. Road rage, checking your appearance, wanting to silence

15

someone you do not agree with and being judgmental is your Izzie brain functioning. Izzie works fast, too. Izzie draws conclusions in 200 milliseconds.

You have two higher brains – the mammalian brain which is the emotional brain, and the neocortex which is the intellectual brain. The neocortex is divided into left for linear, analytical thought, and the right for seeing the whole picture. Ideally, all parts of the brain work together to support each other. When that happens, it is called upshifting. When you have upshifted, I call it being in your Pippi-thinking-brain. (Pippi is named after Pippi Longstocking from children's books.)

Izzie represents the first wolf in the story. Pippi is the second wolf.

Izzie speaks using Poison Phrases. Pippi speaks using PowerPhrases.

Izzie will diminish when you stop feeding fear, anger, envy and the other emotions of the first wolf. Pippi will grow when you feed joy, peace, love, hope and the other emotions of the second wolf.

How Do You Feed Pippi?

The Cherokee elder was wise indeed to say that the part of yourself you feed grows stronger in your life. John Nash discovered that his life went from disaster to success when he went on a "mental diet" and chose which perceptions to pay attention to. (A *Beautiful Mind*). You can enhance Pippi and diminish Izzie by going on a "mental diet" as well.

To diminish Izzie's role in your life,
  • Observe your Izzie thoughts rather than indulging or fighting them. The act of detached observation stimulates upshifting.
  • Avoid Izzie conversations such as participating in gossip or negativity. Instead, be a detached observer of Izzie behavior in others. For example, if you watch reality shows, watch from a perspective of asking whether contestants are operating from Izzie or Pippi brain functioning.
  • Become aware of Poison Phrases and avoid using them.

To feed Pippi,
  • Develop a series of statements to repeat to yourself and questions to ask yourself that cause you to upshift. For example, when going through an

emotionally challenging time that triggered my Izzie, I would ask myself if I was safe in the moment. Of course, I always was, and this calmed me.

- Listen to uplifting materials and read uplifting books.
- Practice elevating the tone of conversations with PowerPhrases. It reinforces Pippi when your words cause someone else to upshift.

Diminishing Izzie and feeding Pippi won't eliminate the desire to be nice and nasty at the same time. It won't eliminate the desire to both affirm and affront someone. Instead, you will be increasingly able to upshift and operate from full brain functioning. That will make all the difference, not just for those around you. It will make all the difference for you.

How to Say PowerPhrases

You may be nervous and/or emotional when you first use your PowerPhrases. Do not let it show in your voice! Sound calm, even if you are not. You can do it, especially when you see the great results that come when you remain calm.

Power Tip— Here's a Pointer for Sounding Calm.

Pretend you are asking your listener to pass the butter. Asking for the butter is not highly emotional, right? Your vocal tone is calm. That's the tone to use when you communicate your PowerPhrases.

Be Prepared to Experience Life at a New Level

Whether your habit is to over-express or under-express, be prepared for exciting changes when you communicate with PowerPhrases. I get emails weekly from people who have discovered what a difference it makes when they speak up, speak out and speak well. (Many are available at the end of the book.) Get ready to experience richness in your relationships. That is a natural result of good communication.

The PowerPhrases in this book are here to help you express more of who you are in the world. These are the things you would have said all along, if you had only known how to.

PowerPhrases to the Rescue

I coached a "Sandy" through a tough relationship and divorce. Sandy was intimidated by her domineering spouse. She would be alternately combative and apologetic with him.

One day she called to tell me about how she had communicated her anger with her estranged husband because he had cashed a check that was hers, and kept the money. Sandy was feeling guilty about "hurting" him and about how she expressed her anger. I was sympathetic when we began the conversation, but after she told me what she had said, I informed her that her sympathy was misplaced. Her anger was appropriate and she communicated it responsibly. Sandy was communicating with a new power that was unfamiliar to her. She was frightened by her own power. Her desire to apologize was, in fact, a retreat into a more familiar submissive stance. If you are not used to being your own advocate, PowerPhrases can seem cruel and harsh. If you are accustomed to overreacting, PowerPhrases can seem mushy and soft. Either way requires adjusting to a powerful new way of communicating.

Pippi

Izzie

Learn more about Pippi and Izzie and how they help you *SpeakStrong*
http://www.speakstrong.com/articles/speak-strong/tale.html

CHAPTER 1

PowerPhrases® Defined: What Is a PowerPhrase Anyway?

Let's get some help from the dictionary.

- Power is the ability to get results. Your words have power when they work for you. Target your words for the results you want.
- A phrase is a brief, apt, and cogent expression.

That means a PowerPhrase is an expression that is brief, well-chosen and effective. I describe a PowerPhrase as: a short, specific expression that is focused on results.

Your results come when you say what you mean, mean what you say, and are not being mean when you say it.

It really is that simple. A PowerPhrase is: a short, specific, focused expression that says what you mean and means what you say without being mean when you say it.

Let's get a closer look.

PowerPhrase: A short, specific expression that gets results by saying what you mean, meaning what you say, and not being mean when you say it.

A PowerPhrase Is a SHORT Expression.

- Less is more!

Make your point and stop talking! Forget the detailed explanations that sound like apologies and suggest that you do not have a right to your position. For example, if someone asks you to run for club president and you do not want to, don't say:

— *You know, it is really great that you asked me to serve, and I want to tell you how much I appreciate it! This is the first time anyone has made me an offer like this. Really, ordinarily I would love to, but under the circumstances…*

Instead, use a short **PowerPhrase for Saying No**, such as:

- I'm flattered you asked. My decision is to not serve at this time.
- Thanks for asking. I choose not to serve.
- I would be happy to if I had the time. I make a policy of not over-scheduling myself, and this would overload my schedule.

Martin Luther King, Jr. understood the importance of being brief when he said,

- "I have a dream!"

A longer phrase such as:

— *I have some really good ideas that inspire me and I think you'll want to listen.*

does not carry the impact and is not a PowerPhrase.

PowerPhrases grab your attention and create pictures in your mind.

PowerPhrases Are Specific Expressions.

Their power is in details. Being specific adds impact. Imagine you gave a presentation about a project you are working on. Certainly you would appreciate comments about how great a job you did. However, the comment about the subtlety you used to build expectancy before you detailed your conclusions is the comment you will appreciate the most. By being specific, they showed they were really paying attention.

Being specific limits the possibility of misunderstanding. If I tell you about a dog I see on my hikes, you might imagine a tiny creature or an enormous animal. If I tell you about the Golden Receiver I see on my hikes, your picture is much closer to what I am describing.

PowerPhrases Get RESULTS

Consciously choose what results you want to achieve, and focus your words to make them happen. Set conscious goals. If your conscious mind does not set a goal for the conversation, your unconscious mind will. I am amazed at how often people speak in a way that alienates the very person who can help them. Consider these questions in every conversation you have.

1. How can I get what I want?
2. How do I preserve the relationship while getting what I want?

Weigh both values and choose words that address both.

PowerPhrases Say What You Mean

It sounds simple enough. But don't kid yourself. Do you really say what you mean? Or do you avoid clarity to avoid a reaction? Perhaps you say:

— *That's okay. Don't worry about it.*

A **PowerPhrase for Addressing Conflict** would be more effective. Consider these:

• **This is a problem. We need to find a solution.**

• **This is unacceptable and needs to be addressed.**

• **I need your help to resolve this.**

Do you say what you mean about a problem to everyone but the person you need to tell the most? You are probably so accustomed to editing your thoughts, you are not even aware you do it. Your best PowerPhrases are the direct expressions of your own heart and your own mind. Say what is in there.

I get numerous letters from my newsletter subscribers asking how to communicate in difficult situations. When I respond, they sometimes think I'm some kind of

If your conscious mind does not set a goal for the conversation, your unconscious mind will.

genius. I'm not...I find words for them in what they tell me. Realize that the perfect words are hidden in the last place you are likely to look...in your own heart. The authenticity in your heart is your best source of word power.

Power Pointer— Talk to the Person That You Have the Issue With

Robert came to me with a concern about how his supervisor did not back him up on his decisions. I asked, "What did she say when you talked to her about it?" He replied, "I haven't mentioned it to her." It was easy to tell him what he needed to do.

There are so few role models of how to communicate well. Most sitcoms would not have a story if people would regularly communicate with PowerPhrases. In my fantasy career I will write for nighttime soap operas, and put in some good healthy PowerPhrases. That would present a model of what good communication can look like.

Back up your words with actions.

With PowerPhrases You Mean What You Say!

Your words are only as powerful as your commitment to them. How about you? Do you mean what you say? Or do you say:

- I will...(start the meetings on time whether you are here or not.)

And then when that person is late you wait to begin.

Everyone knows when your deadlines aren't real. Everyone knows when your resistance can be overcome. Everyone knows when you do not intend to follow through!

In the words of Emerson:

- "What you do speaks so loudly I cannot hear a thing you say."

Do not say something unless you intend to back yourself up with action.

This can be hard! Have you ever told a coworker what time you could meet and they pressured you to meet with them immediately? What did you do? Yield to their pressure or stand firm with what you said? Back your words up with actions. If the guilt monster starts whispering recriminations in your ear, remind yourself that your needs are important too.

Power Pointer— Mean What You Say

Claudia consistently would tell her boss how important it was to her to leave work on time, and she told him what she needed from him in order to complete her work by the end of her work day. Her boss ignored her requests and Claudia stayed late to make sure everything was completed.

Then Claudia had a change in childcare that made it impossible for her to stay more than fifteen minutes past the time she was scheduled to leave. Her boss was upset the first time she left before the work was complete, but he quickly learned that now Claudia meant what she said about leaving on time. Miraculously, now that there was a cost to him of not getting things to her, he began to get her what she needed so that she was able to complete her work by end of the business day.

PowerPhrases are as powerful as your commitment to them.

PowerPhrases Avoid Being Mean

Are you being mean in your choice of words? Don't be so sure that you're not. Here are some communication tactics to watch out for. PowerPhrases (1) avoid sarcasm, (2) overkill, (3) assumption of guilt and (4) an attempt to overpower the other person with wit.

1. PowerPhrases Avoid Sarcasm.

— Look who decided to show up...

is NOT a PowerPhrase.

• **When you come late it throws my schedule off for the rest of the day. How can I help you get here on time?**

is a PowerPhrase.

PowerPhrases avoid being mean.

Sarcasm is indirect. PowerPhrases are direct. Sarcasm mocks the listener. PowerPhrases honor the listener. One definition of sarcasm is "the tearing of flesh." Is that what you really want to do?

2. PowerPhrases Avoid Overkill.

A PowerPhrase is as strong as it needs to be and no stronger. A PowerPhrase does not shoot a cannon when a BB would work. For example:

• **Absolutely not!**

can be a PowerPhrase, but only when a gentler version such as:

• **Not this time. Thanks for asking.**

does not work.

I recently had a conversation with a woman who blasted a coworker for speaking too loudly on a personal conversation. It didn't occur to her to simply ask her to speak more softly. Use the appropriate amount of power.

3. PowerPhrases Avoid Assumption of Guilt.

PowerPhrases assume positive intentions unless it is proven otherwise. Don't be too quick to judge! The woman whose coworker was speaking loudly assumed her coworker was aware of how disturbing it was, and simply didn't care. She was incorrect in her assumption.

Avoid the accusative voice of "you" language. Say:

• **I am getting angry.**

Rather than:

— *You make me so mad!*

Say:

• **I was promised a commission structure six months ago and I still do not have one. If this is not resolved I will...**

rather than:

— *You lied!*

4. PowerPhrases Avoid Attempts to Outsmart the Other Person With Wit.

This can be hard! If the other person is behaving in an offensive way, it is tempting to attempt to outsmart them. Avoid the temptation.

If the boss asks "What kind of idiot are you?" you might be tempted to say:

— *The same kind of idiot as the person who hired me.*

— *You tell me. You are the obvious expert.*

Are they clever responses? Yes. Are they PowerPhrases? No. People who use PowerPhrases speak to obtain powerful results. Instead, use the PowerPhrase:

• **When you ask, "What kind of idiot are you?" I find it insulting. I prefer you offer solutions when I make mistakes.**

PowerPhrases avoid the assumption of guilt.

25

> ### *Power Tip— Speak up EARLY!*
>
> *When you express yourself as soon as things become a problem, you minimize the likelihood that you will overreact.*
>
> *Kris and Carol were on a team in a job that required them to set up displays. Kris thought Carol always undid any display she arranged and she resented it. Carol didn't know there was a problem until the end of a week of working together when she overheard an indirect remark Kris made to someone else. She was surprised to discover what a villain she had become!*
>
> *Because Kris hadn't spoken up, what began as a few rearranged display items became an issue of power and control. We have all done this. Speak up early!*

When you speak up as soon as things become a problem, you minimize the likelihood that you will overreact.

Exercise — The PowerPhrase Questions

Now that you understand the characteristics of PowerPhrases, practice the exercises below. Then read Chapter 2 to see how PowerPhrases can overcome Poison Phrases.

PowerPhrase wisdom says, before you speak, ask yourself:

1. Is it short?
2. Is it specific?
3. Is it focused?
4. Does it truly say what I mean?
5. Do I intend to back my words with action?
6. Am I being kind in my choice of words?

List your favorite phrases below.

_____

_____

_____

Next, apply the above questions to your phrases.

If all of your answers are yes, your phrases are PowerPhrases! If you get any "nos," find a better expression in the chapters of this book.

For example, a common phrase among teenagers is "Whatever."

1. Is it short? Yes!
2. Is it specific? No. It carries little information.
3. Is it focused to get positive results? No. It is likely to create resentment and resistance.
4. Does it truly say what you mean? It conveys very little information.
5. Do you intend to back the message up with action? The message does not imply a clear position to back up.
6. Are you being kind in your choice of words? No. Usually this expression is intended sarcastically.

Eliminate the powerless phrases and fill your vocabulary with PowerPhrases. Read on to chapter 2 for more tools in recognizing what PowerPhrases are, by examining what they are not.

Bunny Bubbles tells you what not to say in:
The Center for Lowered Expectations
http://www.speakstrong.com/video/bunnybubbles.html

CHAPTER 2

Poison Phrases and the PowerPhrases® to Overcome Them

Learn to recognize a PowerPhrase when you hear it, and know the difference between PowerPhrases and Poison Phrases. There are nine types of Poison Phrases. They are 1) Filler Poison Phrases, 2) Indecisive Poison Phrases, 3) Deflective Poison Phrases, 4) Negative Poison Phrases, 5) Absolute Poison Phrases, 6) Victim Poison Phrases, 7) Vague Hinting Poison Phrases, 8) Emotional Poison Phrases and, 9) Passive Poison Phrases.

These phrases weaken your words and rob you of respect. They need to be eliminated from your vocabulary.

There are nine types of poison phrases.

1. Avoid Filler Poison Phrases

Qualifiers, hedges and softener phrases weaken your message. Anything you say that does not add to your message makes it weaker. Avoid the following phrases:

— *Well...*

— *Sort of...*

— *I just...*

— *I would tend to...*

— *I guess...*

— I kind of…

— You know…

— I'm wondering if…

— I'm not sure about this but…

— I could be wrong but…

— This is just my opinion, but…

— Sorry to bother you but…

Tag phrases also weaken your messages. Tag phrases are expressions that you tack on to the end of what you say that turn your statement into a question. For example, if you say:

• **This is the best proposal…**

and you follow with:

— You know?

— Isn't it?

— Right?

— Do you see?

you imply that you are not sure and need the other person's verification. Other weakening tags are:

— Aren't you?

— Doesn't it?

— Won't you?

If the statement really is a question, follow the statement with a clear and direct question.

Also, eliminate all words that do not add useful information. Kind of like… you know?

Tag phrases weaken your messages.

Power Pointer— Join Toastmasters International

To eliminate filler words, attend Toastmasters International meetings. When you speak, someone will count the number of filler words that you use. Most people are quite surprised to learn how many ums and uhs they use. Becoming conscious is the first step in making a change. Initially people get very self-conscious about having their filler words counted, but gradually the habit is broken.

---

2. Replace Indecisive Poison Phrases With Decisive PowerPhrases

Speak with certainty and decisiveness. If you cannot be certain on one position, express what you can be certain about.

Speak with certainty and decisiveness.

Avoid	Replace with
I should…	I will…
I'll try…	I will…
I might be able to…	What I can commit to is…
I sort of think…	I know…
It's just my opinion…	I believe…
I would tend to think…	I think…
You might want to consider…	I recommend…

Trust yourself! Speak what you know with confidence. If your words express doubt, your listener will doubt you no matter how true your words are.

PowerPhrases to the Rescue

I have an email friendship with a dear old friend who is quite successful in his career. We agreed that we wanted to have a phone conversation and he would tell me "I'll try to call you next week." When the phone call didn't come I would fill him in on my upcoming schedule. Once again he would promise to "try" to call but the call never came. This happened several times.

I was reluctant to confront him about it, because I saw him as important and busy. I was afraid I might anger him. When I noticed I felt undervalued I realized I needed to speak. I said:

- I would rather forget about our having a phone conversation, than for you to say that you will try, and then have it not happen. I feel let down and undervalued, as if our friendship is not important to you. Let's not talk about speaking on the phone until you are able to tell me what you WILL do rather than what you will TRY to do.

He responded with an apology and a firm commitment to a day and time, which he upheld. We had a wonderful conversation. I was reminded of the power of asking for what I want—and the power of "I will" rather than "I'll try."

Learn the power of "I will" rather than "I'll try."

3. Replace Poison Phrases That Deflect Due Credit and Replace Them With PowerPhrases That Accept Due Credit

When was the last time you deflected a compliment? Yesterday? I am not suggesting you brag. Bragging does not impress anyone–but neither does false modesty.

Avoid	Replace with
I got lucky.	I worked hard.
It was nothing…	Thanks for noticing.
This old thing?	Thank you.
Anyone could have…	I'm pleased with the outcome too.

When you deflect a compliment, you refuse a gift. Accept their gifts and do not play small.

People who practice positive personal public relations are the first to get ahead. People who play down their accomplishments undermine their own success.

Power Pointer— Accept Due Credit

Did you know that women are far more likely to deflect compliments and credit for their accomplishments than men are?

I saw this point illustrated when I was receiving cranial sacral treatment from a husband/wife team. (Cranial sacral is a type of bodywork.) When I came for the second treatment, the husband asked what results I had experienced from the first one. I said it seemed like it was a good thing to do. He asked if my shoulder pain was better, and I replied that it was, but I had thought that was due to not having been on the computer. He and his wife spoke simultaneously. He said, " I think we deserve credit for that." At the exact same moment his wife said "Oh, that's probably it."

Accept credit when due!

Bragging does not impress anyone— but neither does false modesty.

4. Replace Negative Poison Phrases With Positive PowerPhrases

Be careful of Negative Poison Phrases. You know the ones. They get you so focused on what you do not want that that's all you can think about. That leaves no room for what you want!

Your mind makes sense of positives more easily than negatives. Put your focus on what you want, not on what you do not want. Talk about how you will solve a problem or what you learned from a mistake more than you talk about the problem. Draw attention to your strengths, and take the emphasis off your weaknesses.

Your mind makes sense of positives more easily than negatives.

Avoid	Replace with
Everything went wrong…	I learned from some setbacks.
I'll have to…	I'll be glad to…
I can't…	What I can do is…
I am spending time…	I am investing time…
I'm no good at…	I'm getting better at…
You'll have to excuse…	Here it is…
If only I had…	Starting now I will…
This is bad…	What good can we get out of this?
I can't get to this until…	I can get to this by…
Don't forget to…(log off of your computer.)	Be certain to…(log off of your computer.)

Any time you find yourself ready to express a negative, ask yourself what the upside is and speak from that perspective.

Power Thinking— Think in the Positive

One day as I was walking up to address a group in Amarillo, Texas, I was thinking,

— *"Don't call it armadillo. Don't call it armadillo."*

When I opened my mouth what came out was,

— *"I am delighted to be here in armadillo."*

My subconscious did not register the "don't," and armadillo was imprinted on my brain. Next time I will remind myself of what I DO want to say.

• It's Amarillo.

---

5. Replace Absolute Poison Phrases and Labels With Accurate PowerPhrases

You lose credibility when you speak in sweeping generalizations and absolutes. Stick to the facts! "Always" and "never" are generalizations that are rarely factual.

You lose credibility when you speak in sweeping generalizations and absolutes.

Avoid	Replace with
You always…	On several occasions you have…
I never…	Up until now I have not…
Everything…	Many things…
You're lazy.	Your performance is not up to standard.
You are incompetent.	There are several mistakes here that need to be fixed.

Support your assertions with specific examples.

6. Replace Victim Poison Phrases With PowerPhrases That Place Responsibility and Emphasis Where It Is Due

You do not score points or gain credit for indicating that you are someone else's victim.

— *Poor me!*

is not a PowerPhrase. Any statement that inappropriately places responsibility on others is not a PowerPhrase either. Avoid saying:

— *You make me so mad.*

— *You make me feel wonderful!*

Those phrases imply you have no control over your own emotions. You don't want to send that message. Avoid implying that you do not have the ability to choose alternative thoughts and behaviors.

You may have heard it suggested that you should replace accusative sounding "you" statements with "I" statements, such as:

• **I feel angry when you...**

• **I feel wonderful when you...**

If you make your feelings the subject when the real subject is something else, you sound immature and childish.

These statements avoid placing responsibility for the emotion on the other person. While that is good, there can be a problem in that they make *your feelings* the subject of the communication. If you make your feelings the subject when the real subject is something else, you sound immature and childish. If the subject of your communication is your anger or wonderful feelings, the above statements are appropriate and accurate PowerPhrases. If the subject is something else, the above statements are not PowerPhrases.

If the point you want to make is that Joe's tardiness causes you all kinds of problems, do not make Joe or yourself the subject of the communication. Rather than saying:

— *You make me mad when you come late.*

or:

— *I get angry when you are late.*

Use a **PowerPhrase to Place Responsibility and Emphasis Where It Is Due**, such as:

• **Starting late causes serious problems which we need to address.**

Do not say:

— *Traffic made me late. (Accusatory. The traffic may not care, but you do not sound powerful.)*

Instead use a **PowerPhrase to Place Responsibility and Emphasis Where It Is Due**, such as:

• **There was more traffic than I allowed for.**

Do not say:

— *You are not being clear. (Accusatory)*

— *I am not following you. (Makes you the subject.)*

Instead use a **PowerPhrase to Place Responsibility and Emphasis Where It Is Due**, such as:

• **Please clarify this point.**

• **That last point is not clear to me.**

Simply ask yourself what you are really talking about, and make that the subject.

7. Replace Hints and Vague Poison Phrases With Specific PowerPhrases

It's unfortunate and true that people cannot read your mind. Have you ever hinted to someone and then been upset because they did not take your hint? Be straightforward and specific about what you want. You have only yourself to blame if people do not respond to your vague requests.

Be straightforward and specific about what you want.

Avoid	Replace with
I sure wish someone would...	Will you...
I'd like to have something like...	I want ___ by___ because___.
You need to do a better job.	Your performance needs to be improved. Here are the criteria for acceptable performance. Number one...

Do you hint at things in order to avoid risking rejection? If you never clearly ask, you will never be turned down! Powerful people are willing to risk rejection for the sake of clarity and effectiveness.

8. Avoid Emotional Poison Phrases in Business Situations Where Factual Action-Based PowerPhrases Hold More Power

Stick to information and action phrases.

Your emotions are important. There is power in communicating your emotions, but not to the exclusion of facts and outcomes. When you emphasize information and action phrases, it adds to your credibility.

Avoid	Replace with
I feel great about this proposal.	This proposal will improve our bottom line by ___.
I don't like this idea.	There are three serious problems with this idea. First...
I am angry about this delay.	How do you plan to get back on schedule after this delay?

Know what you feel. Find people to communicate your frustrations and hurts to. Express your emotions when relevant. Then accentuate PowerPhrases that are factual and action-based.

9. Avoid Passive Poison Phrases and Replace With Active PowerPhrases

What is wrong with the following sentence?

"The acquisition contract was signed by the CFO."

This statement is in the passive voice. You can tell a passive sentence by the inclusion of "was," which is a form of the verb "to be." This sentence starts with the contract, even though the CFO is the one acting and should be the subject. To be in the active voice, the sentence needs to begin with the one acting.

Avoid	Replace with
The acquisition contract was signed by the CFO.	The CFO signed the acquisition contract.
The bone was buried by the dog.	The dog buried the bone.

The passive voice sounds...well...passive, which weakens your message.

Overcome Poison Phrases With PowerPhrases

You will develop perceptiveness for PowerPhrases that will work like radar.

Keep your ears open to hear how the principles of this chapter are applied everywhere. When you understand the principles of PowerPhrases and are familiar with the specific applications in other chapters, your ear will work like radar. You will immediately recognize the difference between Poison Phrases and PowerPhrases.

Exercise

Replace the following Poison Phrases with PowerPhrases.

I sort of like this idea.

_____

This is just my opinion, but…

_____

This is great, don't you think?

_____

I might be able to…

_____

It was no big deal.

_____

Don't come late.

_____

This will never work.

_____

You hurt my feelings.

_____

I wish I didn't have to go to the meeting alone.

_____

I'm excited about this account.

_____

The suspect was apprehended.

_____

CHAPTER 3

PowerPhrases® for Saying "No"
"No" IS a Complete Sentence – But Is It a PowerPhrase®?

You've just been asked for a loan. Someone needs a day off and you can't spare them. Your coworker wants you to do their work for them. Why can't you just say a simple...

• "No"?

"No" is so short, so simple, and so powerful. "No" also can be so frightening. When was the last time you agreed to something because you were afraid to say no?

According to informal polls I conduct, two-thirds of the population has trouble with that little two-letter word! PowerPhrases make saying "no" easier.

Nancy Reagan knew the importance of having the right words to say when she began an anti-drug campaign based on the slogan "Just say:

Two-thirds of the population has trouble saying no.

• No!"

to drugs. Other phrases such as:

• "NO is a complete sentence!"

and

• "What part of NO don't you understand?"

evolved from this campaign.

While powerful, these phrases are flat refusals. Flat refusals carry risk and are often inappropriate.

A flat refusal can brand you as rude and uncooperative.

A flat refusal may be interpreted as discrediting the request or offer. While a flat refusal does say what it means and mean what it says, it can come across as being hostile.

PowerPhrases use the amount of power required and no more. Start your "no" gently and work your way up if necessary.

There are three steps for saying no.

The Three-Step Process for Saying "No"

When You Refuse a Request, ACT!

1. **Acknowledge** their request.

Say something to recognize their request. Make a short comment to let them know that you heard them and you are considering what they said.

A flat refusal can brand you as rude and uncooperative.

2. Clarify your **Circumstance.**

Tell them a little bit about your own situation. Be brief. Mention what it is that keeps you from being able to honor their request.

3. **Transform** your refusal into a positive. Suggest alternatives or make a comment that reaffirms the relationship such as:

• **Some other time.**

Put them all together and you have a three-step "no."

• **It sounds like a great idea. Unfortunately I have other priorities. Perhaps next time I can.**

Read on for further options for each of the three steps.

Step 1: Acknowledge — PowerPhrases to Acknowledge the Request

- I understand this is important.
- Ordinarily I would love to help.
- I appreciate you thinking of me.
- Thanks for asking.
- I wish I could help out here.
- I am aware...
- What a great idea!
- I am flattered you asked.
- I understand your situation. I have been there myself.

Step 2: Circumstances — PowerPhrases to Explain Circumstances

- My situation is...
- My policy is...
- I have plans.
- I'm not up to it.
- I'm not the best person for this job.
- I'm not available.
- I have commitments.
- It doesn't work for me.
- My circumstances make it impossible.
- After realizing the scope...
- I choose not to.
- I will pass on this opportunity.
- I am responsible for...

When you refuse a request, ACT!

Step 3: Transform — PowerPhrases to Transform the Refusal by Reaffirming the Relationship or Offering Alternatives

• Perhaps next time.

• Thanks again for asking.

• I hope you can find the help you need.

• I wish I could.

• While I can't do what you are asking, what I can do is...

• Here's an alternative...

• Have you considered...?

• Have you tried asking Judy? (While this might work for you, it also might not make you very popular with Judy.)

• I _can_ help you by...

If you can't or don't want to give them what they want, look for an alternative that is acceptable to you.

Liberated by a Two-Letter Word and Some Good Healthy Power Thinking

I was on a team with "Mike," whom I found to be controlling. It seemed to me that I was constantly giving in, but I did not worry about it because the issues were small and I was able to go along. That changed when Mike expected me to split a bill that was his responsibility. Although it was only an issue of about five dollars, I knew that if I paid it, I would not feel good about myself.

I used the ACT formula and stood my ground. He was quite used to getting his way, and became visibly upset when I did not cave in to his pressure. After I "ACTed" him four times, he paid the bill and we walked down the hallway in silence. He was bristly and cold, and I was thinking:

> — *Oh Meryl, what have you done? Now he will be impossible to work with. Am I being picky? It's not that much money.*

Then I heard myself and I said to myself:

> • **Meryl, you have a habit of being unhappy when other people are upset with you. Get over it!**

In that moment I was free. He was unhappy with me— and I was quite pleased with myself. I see bondage as being constrained by other people's opinions of us. Freedom is being our own judge and jury.

Later that day Mike did something else that I thought was outrageous, and I "ACTed" once more. Now it was becoming easier.

Not everyone will appreciate your use of PowerPhrases. Don't let that stop you. You will appreciate yourself.

Freedom is being our own judge and jury.

45

ACT Now! Put the Three-Step Process for Saying "No" Together to Get Complete PowerPhrases.

Combine one phrase from each of the three categories to make a complete and effective **PowerPhrase for Saying "No"** without caving in and without losing friends.

Say"No" without caving in and without losing friends.

Acknowledge	Circumstances	Transform
I understand this is important.	My situation is ...	Perhaps next time.
Ordinarily I would love to help.	My policy is ...	Thanks for asking.
I appreciate you thinking of me.	I have other plans...	I'm sure you'll find the right person you need.
I would if I could.	I have other involvements.	Have you considered..?
I wish I could help out here.	I'm not well-suited to do what you want.	Here's an option...
I see you need help.	After looking at my calendar I see I can't give you the help you need.	Have you considered asking ___?
I'm honored that you thought of me.	After realizing the scope of the request, I choose to pass.	I wish you success.

Avoid being wordy. Here's what you don't want to sound like:

— *Gosh, I am so sorry, I really hate to tell you this because it sounds like you could use some help and I would love to help you if I could. If only the circumstances were different, but I have to take my daughter to little league and last time I missed a game I felt just awful because (etc.)...*

The more details you give, the weaker you sound and the more inclined they will be to argue.

Sometimes they will argue even when you are clear and direct. In these cases, use only two of the three parts to add strength to your "no."

Saying "No" in Two Parts

When you say no in two parts, it sounds stronger. Some people's sensitivity causes them to hear the slightest hint of "no" as a personal rejection and they need a softer version. Use all three steps for them. Others do not take it as personally, and a two-part no works well.

There are some people that will argue with and attempt to manipulate anything we say. A two-part no works better with these.

The more details you give, the weaker you sound and the more inclined they will be to argue.

The Two-Step Process for Saying "No"

Acknowledge	Circumstances	Transform
I'd love to.	However, I am busy.	
Thanks for asking.	Not this time.	
	My boss has already scheduled my time.	If you want, you can ask her.
Sounds interesting.	I have other commitments.	
	I have a 3:00 deadline.	I wish I could.

> ### Power Thinking to the Rescue
>
> *What are you telling yourself that keeps you from saying "no"? Don't think:*
>
> — *If I say no, they may not like me.*
>
> — *I better be nice.*
>
> — *I shouldn't say what I think.*
>
> *Instead, use Power Thinking. Think:*
>
> • **What are my true priorities?**
>
> • **What response best serves my true priorities?**
>
> • **How can I communicate that as graciously and effectively as possible?**
>
> *People who are comfortable saying no are usually people who have a clear idea of what their priorities are. Use Power Thinking to remind you of yours.*

People who are comfortable saying no are usually people who have a clear idea of what their priorities are.

When a Simple "NO" Is a PowerPhrase

As you recall, a PowerPhrase is as strong as it needs to be, and no stronger. A PowerPhrase does not shoot a cannon when a BB would work. In addition, a PowerPhrase assumes good intentions unless it is proven otherwise.

The fact is, sometimes people simply do not get the message on the first communication. Stronger PowerPhrases can be called for when:

1. The listener is unusually direct,
2. The listener is manipulative or a "taker," or
3. The listener hears acknowledgement as uncertainty or as an opening.

For example, Jan is naturally very direct. She expects and appreciates directness from others. Jan appreciates a flat no. She does not want to take the time to hear all the reasons. "No" is a PowerPhrase for her.

Roberta is a nurse who works in a hospital. She will take advantage of others when they allow it. None of the staff enjoy working weekends, but it is a supportive environment where people pitch in for each other. When Roberta asked Jan to take her weekend shift, Jan assumed Roberta had a great need, and agreed. She felt used when she later discovered that Roberta did not have anything special happening, she simply did not want to work weekends. The next time Roberta asked her to cover her shift, Jan said:

Acknowledge	Circumstances	Transform
I am aware you don't enjoy working weekends.	My family likes me home weekends as well. My policy is to cover for people only when they have emergencies.	

A PowerPhrase is as strong as it needs to be, and no stronger.

That statement is a PowerPhrase; strong, clear and direct.

Roberta started having a lot of "emergencies." Jan used another approach. She tried to turn the "no" into a negotiation by saying:

Acknowledge	Circumstances	Transform
I understand you don't want to work weekends.	I will be happy to cover for you again after you have covered a weekend for me.	

Although Jan was being strong, clear and direct, Roberta saw it as an opportunity to argue. "Well, I did cover for you a couple of weekdays in trade for your weekend. I wanted to cover for you the other weekend, but you didn't want to take that weekend off." Jan realized that with Roberta, her PowerPhrase was to just say:

- **No.**

or

- **No, I do not want to.**

and to refuse to discuss it any further. Roberta tested Jan's no: Jan had to repeat it several times. Eventually Roberta gave up—and found someone else to take advantage of. If you have ever tried to assert yourself with someone who argues with any explanation you give, you probably already know that with these people it is best to avoid explanations that give them something to argue about.

Turning Your NO Into a Negotiation

Sometimes, rather than completely refusing a request or offer, suggest alternatives.

Sometimes, rather than completely refusing a request or offer, you can suggest alternatives. For example, when one assistant was asked to make copies, she said she would love to but she had a huge stack of orders to file. Then she used the PowerPhrase:

- **I'll do it if you'll...(help file orders).**

Another assistant's boss gave her an assignment that would require her full attention. She said:

Acknowledge	Circumstances	Transform
I know this project is top priority.	In order to meet the deadline I need to have uninterrupted time.	I can do this if you'll answer the phones.

Her supervisor answered the phones for her for two weeks, because it was necessary to get the job done.

Many business people know how to say "no" to their bosses without ever using the word. When a supervisor makes a request that conflicts with a previous request, they will reply:

Acknowledge	Circumstances	Transform
I know this is important.	I am working on the XYZ account.	Which is the priority?
		What can I put aside to make time to complete this?

PowerPhrases That Buy You Time

If you are a chronic yes-sayer, you can overcome the yes habit by using a PowerPhrase to delay long enough to plan your response.

Delay phrases lack the power of a clear refusal, but are superior to a yes when you do not mean it. Learn the **PowerPhrases for Buying Time.**

- Let me get back to you.
- I need to check on a few things before answering you.
- I need to give this consideration before responding.
- Let me think about it and let you know.
- I'll see what I can do and tell you tomorrow.

When you use these, be sure to mean what you say. Check on, consider or think about it, and get back to them rather than letting the request remain unresolved.

When They Ask, "Will You Do Me a Favor?"

What do you say when someone asks you to agree before telling you what the request is? Avoid saying:

— *Sure.*

Instead, use a **PowerPhrase for Getting Clarification Before Agreeing,** such as:

- What do you need?
- I just might! What is it?

A chronic yes–sayer can overcome the habit by using PowerPhrases to buy time.

- Tell me what and I'll see.
- I need to know what the favor is before I can answer you.

PowerPhrases to the Rescue—Before You Agree...

When I train assistants I share a story about a woman who was an assistant for a VP in her company. At a convention, the CEO of the company came to her and said, "Wouldn't it be nice if we had hats with the company logo embroidered on them for all 650 employees this evening? Please take care of that."

The CEO had never made a request of this woman before, so he was not aware of her history of excellence.

Her response was to say, "I have no idea of how I could possibly do that." That response had negative repercussions for her.

At seminars I have my groups explore options. Some ask for clarification of budget, quality specifications and if the evening meeting is an absolute deadline. Others ACT by acknowledging the great idea, explaining why they believe it might not be possible and suggesting alternatives. Still others buy time, and say:

- **Let me check on a few things and get back to you.**

Learning to say no does not mean that we ignore the sensitivities of the other person. It does mean that we also respect our own requirements.

Learning to say no does not mean that we ignore the sensitivities of the other person.

EXERCISES

I. You have been asked to do something that falls outside of your direct line of work and expertise. How do you refuse the assignment?

Step 1:

Acknowledge the request.

_____

Step 2:

Explain **Circumstances.**

_____

Step 3:

Transform the refusal into a positive by reaffirming the relationship or suggesting an alternative.

_____

II. Someone is taking a collection for a birthday gift for an employee you don't know. You are on a tight budget. How do you refuse?

Step 1:

Acknowledge the request.

_____

Step 2:

Explain **Circumstances.**

_____

Step 3:

Transform the refusal into a positive by reaffirming the relationship or suggesting an alternative.

_____

The Power of NO

The Beatles wrote a song that contains the following lines: "I ain't no fool and I don't take what I don't want." Every time you say "yes" to something you don't want, you are saying "no" to what you do. As with any habit, overcoming the "yes" habit will be uncomfortable. Say no anyway! Take a deep breath and use the "butter" voice that was described in the introduction. Whatever you do, do not take your words back because you are outside of your comfort zone.

I often meet people who used to say yes, and have since discovered the power of no. They found it a challenge at first, but incredibly rewarding. They always smile when they tell me about saying no, because the small and powerful word helps them take control and sets them free. These PowerPhrases will help YOU take control and they will set you free.

Sometimes you just gotta say "no."
Watch *The Legend of Mighty Mouth* to learn more.
http://www.speakstrong.com/video/mightymouth.swf

CHAPTER 4

PowerPhrases® That Transform Conflicts Into Understanding

What words come to mind when you think of conflict? Write four below.

_____ _____

_____ _____

My audiences often pick words like anger, frustration, shouting, and tension. What do these words have in common? They are all negative! Can you think of some positive words that apply to conflict? Write four below.

_____ _____

_____ _____

Was that a bit harder? It usually is. It is challenging to think of words like breakthrough, understanding, and resolution. You have to train yourself to think Power Thoughts and to speak PowerPhrases in conflict. Negative words and statements that intensify the conflict come more easily.

It will help if you view conflict as a natural and healthy aspect of life and relationships. This attitude helps you become more willing to air your differences at earlier stages, and that makes resolution much easier.

Train yourself to think Power Thoughts and to speak PowerPhrases in conflict.

Think: "There is a solution here."

Power Thinking to the Rescue

Pay attention to your thoughts when conflict begins. Avoid thinking:

— I better avoid this disagreement.

— I can't handle conflict.

— Who do they think they are?

Instead, choose Power Thoughts, such as:

- There is a solution here.
- Conflict is a normal part of life and we will get to the other side.
- I can stay calm and express myself gracefully.
- What do I want? What do they want? How can we resolve this?

About a year ago, I was contracted by the Department of Defense to do three days of conflict management training. The entire division was called in for the training because a few men had had incidences of violence. None of them wanted to be there. They tried to get the unions to stop the training. This was the most hostile group I have ever faced.

I had to be very assertive with myself about my thinking. I was tempted to think:

— This is going to be awful!

— I want out of here!

— I can't handle this.

Every time I had a thought like that, I chose to replace the thought with Power Thoughts such as:

- I am very good at what I do.
- This is an opportunity.

> • They are going to be very glad that this training was mandatory.
>
> *By the end they were glad to have been there. I had Power Thinking to thank.*

Conflict is a very hot topic! Do you want to know how to get that other person to shape up? Do you want to know exactly what to say to put others in their place? This chapter will not tell you either. What it <u>will</u> do is tell you exactly what to say to keep from being the source of the problem, and give you concrete steps and phrases to use to resolve the problems that do occur.

When conflicts arise, you must know how to make your CASE! That means:

Clarify their position,

Assert your position,

Seek solutions and

Evaluate options and create agreements.

When conflicts arise, make your CASE.

Make your CASE Step 1: Clarifying Their Position

Do you ever jump to conclusions in conflict situations? Do you imagine that they are doing awful things on purpose? Do you think they are out to get you? If so, you are normal! We all become self-focused, and reach conclusions before clear evidence is obtained. Develop a habit of standing in the other person's shoes. Clarify their perspective before asserting your own.

Dr. Stephen Covey says to:

• "Seek first to understand and then to be understood."

Adopt this motto—with one addition.

• Seek first to understand, and make it clear to them that you do. Then seek to be understood.

It is not enough that you understand the other person. They need to feel understood. Remember that:

• No one cares how much you know until they know how much you care.[1]

Power Listening to the Rescue

The meeting was getting nowhere. Sheila was on the defensive. Whatever people said was considered to be a personal affront.

Finally I said:

• Let's listen to Sheila and tell her our understanding of what she is saying until we are certain and she is certain that we are hearing her.

The suggestion worked like magic. Sheila relaxed and spoke from a position of being open and vulnerable. Surprisingly, once she had the floor, she only needed to speak a short while. Then she was open to hearing what we had to say.

It is not enough that you understand the other person. They need to feel understood.

You will get excellent results when you demonstrate interest and concern as the first step in managing conflict. Explore your assumptions by asking questions. Ask your questions gracefully. Watch out for set-up questions like:

— *Why...?*

— *Why don't you ever...?*

— *Why do you always...?*

"Why" questions tend to put the other person on the defensive.

[1] Cavett Robert, Founder, National Speakers Association.

Also avoid accusative, closed-ended questions that result in defensiveness, such as:

— *Did you do that to sabotage me?*

— *Are you out to get me?*

Instead, use a **PowerPhrase to Ask Clarifying Questions,** such as:

• Help me to understand…

• Let me make sure I understand you clearly…

• Are you aware…? (I LOVE this one!)

• Your intentions are not clear to me. Can you help me out here?

• What did you mean by…?

Power Pointer— Listen With Your Heart

I believe that to understand all is to forgive all. It is easy to find the flaw in other people's thinking. It is harder to find out how it makes sense to them. Listen to learn about them. Listen to understand all. As long as you have judgments, you do not truly understand.

The good news is that you can listen to yourself in the same way. Listen to yourself and others with your heart.

If you are judging yourself or others, think:

• There is something I do not understand here.

• There is a reason that they are behaving this way.

To understand all is to forgive all.

Many of their answers will probably anger or upset you. Consider their words and explore their position more thoroughly before asserting your own. Do not let your reaction stand in the way of managing conflict successfully. Instead, keep listening to them, and continue to seek to understand. It won't help you to say:

— *That is a ridiculous idea!*

— *You are kidding, right?*

— *How could you possibly think that?*

— *You're wrong!*

Instead, use a **PowerPhrase to Acknowledge Without Agreeing**, such as:

• I see. Tell me more.

• This is a big issue for you.

• I might feel that way if I was in your shoes.

• That's an interesting perspective.

• I did not realize that you felt that way.

• I had not considered that perspective.

• Please continue.

• That may be.

• I appreciate your sharing your experience. What else do I need to know?

At various intervals, use **PowerPhrases to Ask Questions That Confirm Understanding**, such as:

• This is my understanding of what you are saying... What do I still need to know to understand your perspective?

• What I hear you saying is... Is my understanding correct?

Redirect any urge you may have to scream, curse or throw cold water on them, into effective conflict management. Continue to use **PowerPhrases to Ask Clarifying Questions, PowerPhrases to Acknowledge Without Agreeing**, and **PowerPhrases to Ask Questions That Confirm Understanding** until it is clear that you understand them, and they know it. Most people do not make it this far!

It is easy to find the flaw in other people's thinking. It is harder to find out how it makes sense to them.

Power Pointer— Pick Your Battles

Always be aware of your chances of success when you decide what to address.

Following a merger, my client Donna found herself reporting to a manager who knew far less than she did. The manager decided to relocate the call center to another state because "cost would be less." Donna was more familiar with the numbers than her supervisor was. Donna knew that although wages were lower, cost per dollar ordered was much higher. The decision was already made, so rather than arguing about something that could not be changed, Donna set her focus on what could be affected. She said:

- You are right that wages are lower there. However, cost per dollar ordered is higher. Let's get some trainers in there to increase their efficiency.

Pick battles small enough to win and big enough to matter.

Pick battles small enough to win and big enough to matter.

When you listen first, people are much more willing to listen to you.

PowerPhrases to the Rescue

An assistant at one of my seminars named Marcie was the representative of a very difficult client. She said that she had his account because she was the only one who could tolerate him at all. After learning how to make her CASE, Marcie prepared a script to request better treatment from him. She began by saying:

- I believe that I understand how you want to be treated as my client. May I go through my understanding to make sure it is correct?

He agreed and she told him of all the things she understood he wanted from her. When the client agreed that her understanding was appropriate, Marcie said:

- Now I would like five minutes of your time to tell you how I would like to be treated as your representative. Can you offer me that?

He agreed and she went through her lists of requests. For example, she said:

- I would like you to view me as someone who is doing what she can to help you.

- I want to be able to clarify my understandings.

When she finished, the client was quiet for several moments. Then he said, "You deserve a raise and a promotion, and I'm going to get you one." He did! He talked to her boss and the result was that she got a raise and a promotion.

When you listen first, people are much more willing to listen to you.

Make Your CASE Step 2: Assert Your Own Position

When the other person agrees that you understand their position, they will be more open to your explanations. Before you speak, elicit a commitment from them to listen and consider your ideas. Use a **PowerPhrase for Requesting Uninterrupted Time to Express Yourself,** such as:

• **You acknowledge that I understand your position. Will you give me five minutes of uninterrupted time to explain mine?**

• **You have made some valid points that make a lot of sense from where you stand. Please hear me out as I describe how it looks to me.**

• **Are you ready to hear how I see it?**

There are three steps to asserting your position in conflict. (A) Describe the problem, (B) communicate the impact, and (C) request a new behavior.

A. Describe the Problem

Open with a description of what happens or what they do in behavioral terms. This means be neutral and leave out all judgment. Think of yourself as an attorney. Attorneys cannot say:

— *You are out to get me.*

— *Obviously, my assignments are of a low priority to you.*

— *You micromanage.*

— *You never respond to me.*

— *I think you were raised in a barn.*

Attorneys must state facts as facts, and leave out opinions (or be subtle about it when they do not). You need to speak with the same integrity.

When the other person agrees that you understand their position, they will be more open to your explanations.

63

Use **PowerPhrases** for Describing the Negative Behavior, such as:

- When...
- I notice...
- The other day...
- When I... you...

Filled in, these sentence stems can sound like the following:

- When... the time for the meeting regarding the Smith account was changed...
- I notice that... the assignment I gave you was moved to the bottom of your project sign-in sheet.
- The other day... you checked my work 14 times.
- When I spoke... you did not respond.

Do not let anyone talk you out of your own experience.

Power Thinking to the Rescue

Do you ever doubt your own perception when someone disagrees with it? Do not let anyone talk you out of your own experience. Certainly you do want to consider their perspective, but do not let their perspective become more important than your own. It won't help you to say:

— *I must be crazy.*

— *They must be crazy.*

— *I shouldn't be thinking and feeling this way.*

Instead, use Power Thinking, such as:

- I am the authority on my view of the situation.
- They are the authority on their view of the situation.
- They have a right to their opinion, and I have a right to mine.
- I have a right to express my opinion.

B. Communicate the Impact

After describing the offending behavior, express the impact, and your thoughts and feelings about it. Watch out for words like:

— *It messes everything up. (Too vague)*

— *I think you don't trust me. (Blaming)*

Instead, use a **PowerPhrase for Expressing the Impact of a Behavior,** such as:

- **What happens is…**
- **The impact is…**
- **I think…**
- **I feel…** (Consider the cautions for "I think" and "I feel" in Chapter 2 before using them.)
- **The effect is…**

Filled in these can sound like:

- **What happens is… I feel alienated from the team.**
- **The impact is… I do not receive my work on time and I do not present well at the meeting.**
- **I think… I'm not trusted.**
- **I feel… uncomfortable.**
- **The effect is… I get confused and make more mistakes.**

Once they understand the impact of their actions, tell them what you want them to do.

C. Request a New Behavior

Once the impact is clear, tell them what you want them to do. Avoid saying:

— *Do this… (Sounds dictatorial)*

— *Don't do that… (Talk about what you WANT, not what you do not want.)*

— *You need to… (Be very careful of sentences that start with "you." It can sound controlling.)*

Instead, use a **PowerPhrase for Requesting a New Behavior,** such as:

- I need…
- I want…
- What I want to see happen is…
- I prefer…
- What would work better is…
- What needs to happen is…
- I need… to be advised of changes as they occur.
- I want… us to work out a standard system for prioritizing work.
- I prefer… to work on my own, checking in at regularly scheduled intervals.

Put the above steps together and you get the three-step process for asserting your position.

Clearly request the new behavior you desire.

Three-Step Process for Asserting Your Own Position Without Intensifying the Conflict

Problem	Impact: Thoughts/ Feelings/Effect	Request
I sent three inquiries without receiving a response.	I think I am being ignored.	I need a prompt acknowledgement of my inquiries and an indication of when my request will be granted.
My situation is that I have been here for three months and I still do not have a workstation of my own.	I feel frustrated. What happens is I have to carry my materials to wherever I can find a station, and it takes quite a while to sort them out.	My request is that the next time someone leaves, I be given their desk.
When you sell products that were designed for my department...	The effect is that my claims of exclusivity to my clients are invalidated and they lose trust in me.	I need you to stop selling our line. I recommend that you request products to be designed exclusively for your department.
When I speak, I notice you are reading the paper.	I believe that you cannot listen to me and read the paper at the same time.	Please give me your full attention.
The other day you spoke with my staff about turnaround times.	They were upset by the way you addressed them and the standards you expressed. They were so upset that very little work got done that day.	I suggest we meet and find a solution to this problem together.

Assert your own position without intensifying the conflict.

*When you give
people corrective
feedback, the
initial response is
usually defensive.*

PowerPhrases to the Rescue— Addressing an Impossible Manager

Trainer Carolyn Burke was once a sales manager at a major bank. The Vice President of Sales, Sharon, believed in management by intimidation. Sharon created an atmosphere of fear and paranoia for the people that Carolyn supervised. If they did not meet their sales goals, once a month they were on the phone with Sharon, where she would humiliate them in front of their peers. One day, after finding a woman named Carrie at her desk in tears, Carolyn decided that it was time to address the issue. She scripted out what she planned to say and practiced with her husband.

When she was fully prepared, Carolyn introduced the topic by saying:

- Sharon, there's an issue I would like to discuss. Can we meet in the conference room?

Once in the conference room, Carolyn continued by saying:

- Sharon, the other day I came back to the office and Carrie was at her desk in tears. She had just gotten off the phone with you for not meeting her sales goals and she was very upset.

Sharon said, — "She should have been. She wasn't doing her job."

Carolyn acknowledged her without agreeing by saying:

- That may be. May I continue?

- I understand the reason why you have these calls is so we will meet our goals and stay off the phone with you. I think you don't know what happens when we get off the phone with you. When we get off the phone with you, we don't feel like going out and selling. We are devastated. Our self-esteem is so low, we want to crawl under the desk and hide. Sharon, you know so much. Share what you know with us rather than scaring us. That will increase our commissions, which will increase your commissions as well.

Sharon replied, — "Carolyn Burke, don't you EVER tell me how to do my job again. Get out of here!" Carolyn responded by saying:

• I understand you're upset. I've just given you feedback. No one enjoys that. I do believe that when you consider what I've told you, you will realize that it will benefit you as well as us.

Carolyn did not push Sharon to acknowledge what she said at that moment. When we give people corrective feedback, the initial response is usually defensive. Carolyn gave Sharon the information and allowed her time to process it. Carolyn's communication was successful. Sharon never made those calls again. Five years later, when Carolyn was leaving the company, Sharon told her that she respected her for addressing the issue that day.

When you express consequences, it is far better to explain the benefits of cooperating than the costs of non-cooperation.

Whether you get acknowledged or not, you reclaim a bit of yourself every time you communicate well.

D. Consequences

Sometimes you will want to include a fourth step for asserting your position—a consequence. When you express consequences, it is far better to explain the benefits of cooperating than the costs of non-cooperation. However, there is a place for both.

Watch out for words like:

— *Do this or else…(Threatening)*

— If I were you…(Condescending)

— You are forcing me to…(Accusatory)

Instead, use a **PowerPhrase for Explaining Consequences,** such as:

• This will…

• The benefit to you is…

• If this happens again, I will…

• Next time this happens I will…

• What this means for you is…

Combine one phrase from each category to make a complete and effective statement of your position.

Use a PowerPhrase for explaining consequences

The Four-Step Process to Assert Your Position

Problem	Impact: Thoughts/ Feelings/Effect	Request	Consequence
I sent three inquiries without receiving a response.	I think I am being ignored.	I need a prompt acknowledgement of my inquiries and an indication of when my request will be granted.	This will keep me from inundating you with repeated requests.
My situation is that I have been here for three months and I still do not have a workstation of my own.	I feel frustrated. What happens is I have to carry my materials to wherever I can find a station, and it takes quite a while to sort them out.	My request is that the next time someone leaves, I be given their desk.	The benefit to you is I will be more efficient in my work.
When you sell products that were designed for my department...	The effect is that my claims of exclusivity to my clients are invalidated and they lose trust in me.	I need you to stop selling our line. I recommend that you request products to be designed exclusively for your department.	If this happens again I will bring the issue to the supervisor.
When I speak, I notice that you are reading the paper.	I believe that you cannot listen to me and read the paper at the same time.	I want your full attention.	Next time this happens I will wait until I have your full attention to speak.

You can assert your position in one to four steps.

Asserting Your Position in One to Three Steps

While I recommend you decide what you would say for all four steps if you were to use them, sometimes you will want to use shorter statements, omitting some elements.

Problem	Impact: Thoughts/ Feelings/Effect	Request	Consequence
		Please give me your full attention when I speak.	
I have not received a response to the memo I sent last week.			If this continues I will request that you be removed from the project.
		How can I help you get here on time?	
	Clients are threatening to withdraw their accounts.	I need the figures immediately.	

Why not request that you look for solutions together?

Often step one and two of making your case, clarifying their position and asserting your own, are all you need. They will say, "sure, no problem," and you will see if your requests are honored. Sometimes you will either not agree on the problem, or you will not agree on the solution. When that happens, move to step 3, and seek solutions.

Make Your Case Step 3: Seeking Solutions

The best solutions are the ones you decide on together. A great way to start is to request that you look for solutions together. Use a **PowerPhrase to Request That You Negotiate Solutions Together**, such as:

• **What I want to see happen is for us to negotiate solutions together.**

• **I suggest that we kick around a few ideas to see what solutions we can come up with.**

- If we could come up with a solution that works for us both, would you be interested?
- What would it take to make my request possible?
- I believe we can work this out to both of our satisfaction. Will you work with me on this?
- I need your help to resolve this.

Before you can effectively seek solutions, you might need to find a definition of the problem that you both can agree to. In larger issues, it is worth the time to reach a mutual definition of the problem. For example, one of my clients could not get her employee to admit that her actions undermined the team, but she was willing to admit that there was a perception of her not being a team player. They set out to find ways to change the perception. The resulting solutions were effective.

One approach to negotiating solutions is outlined in *How to Deal With Difficult People* by Paul Friedman. It comes from The Federal Mediation and Conciliation Service. It suggests that you both complete the following **PowerPhrases for Seeking Solutions:**

In larger issues, it is worth the time to reach a mutual definition of the problem.

- I think I should...

- You think you should...

- I think you should...

- You think I should...

Find the points of agreement, and combine the lists into:

- We think we should...

Another powerful way for you to generate options is to brainstorm solutions. You can do it on your own, or you can get with the other parties involved and offer solutions until you get 20 options. Let yourself get a little crazy in your ideas. Tell your mental critic's committee that they will get their turn later. You will welcome logic and common sense during the evaluation phase later.

Power Pointer— Brainstorming Solutions

At one company where I was doing conflict resolution training, the group decided to brainstorm solutions to see if they could resolve a problem as a group. They chose to brainstorm solutions for conflict in meetings. The meetings were turning into venting sessions. Management was delighted that the group was taking it on themselves to address the problem, because the meetings were a burden to them too.

We thought of solutions until we got twenty. Some were extreme, but we did not evaluate them until later. We narrowed it to five guidelines to implement, which they all agreed on.

They implemented the guidelines and followed up two weeks later to see what they wanted to keep and what to change. Meetings were transformed, but what was really transformed was the group. They learned that they actually wanted the same things and that they could work together to resolve the problem.

Once you have evaluated your options, make concrete commitments and arrange follow-up.

Make Your Case Step 4: Evaluating Options and Building Agreements

Once you have at least twenty options on paper, review them and see which ones or one you can agree to. For each option, use **PowerPhrases to Evaluate Options,** such as:

- Does this option solve the problem?
- Can you and I both live with this option?
- Is there any way to improve this option?
- Is it realistic?
- Are you and I both willing to commit to it in writing?

Once you evaluate your options, make concrete commitments and arrange follow-up. If they resist and say that obviously you do not trust them, say:

- Putting it in writing ensures we have the same understanding.
- My policy is to get agreements as clear as possible to avoid surprises later.
- Follow-up enables us to review our decisions in case a situation arises that we did not consider.

At follow-up, ask:

- How is it working for you?
- What needs to change?
- Is there anything we did not anticipate?

Power Pointer— Get It In Writing

Years ago when my son was fourteen, we were negotiating everything in our lives together. I asked what he needed from me and talked about what I needed from him. We had been at odds, but this discussion was framed with an understanding that neither one of us would agree to anything we did not feel good about.

When it came time to put the agreement in writing, I noticed that my son became much more serious. He was willing to verbally agree to many things that he was not willing to agree to in writing. Putting it in writing made it much more concrete. It creates a higher level of commitment.

Putting agreements in writing makes the agreement more concrete and creates a higher level of commitment.

Exit Lines

Are you thinking that making your CASE sounds great, but can it be so simple? Of course there are times when they or you get highly emotional and cannot stay calm. Knowing when to *stop* talking is as important as knowing when to *start*. If you are upset and emotional, DO NOT CONTINUE! Instead, use an exit line to remove yourself and give yourself time to gain perspective. Here is what you DON'T want to say:

— *I am out of here...(Too abrupt)*

— *There is no talking to you...(Accusatory)*

— *This is a waste of time... (Negative)*

— *You are an idiot...(Insulting)*

Knowing when to stop talking is as important as knowing when to start.

Instead, use a **PowerPhrase Exit Line,** such as:

• I need to check on some things before continuing this discussion. Let's meet again at...

• I need to take some time to regain perspective before answering you. Let's talk again Friday.

• My policy is not to discuss emotionally charged subjects when I am upset. I need some time now. Let's talk later.

• You deserve respect. Right now, I'm so angry I can't offer you that. I need ____ minutes.[2]

• I'm afraid if we continue this discussion I'll say something I will regret. Let's give it a 24-hour rest.

• I value our work relationship too much to speak when I am as upset as I am now. Let's pick this up tomorrow.

• I think it is possible that one of us might say something we will wish we hadn't. Let's meet later when we are calmer.

One assistant said that once when she was upset with her boss she said:

[2] Carol Scofield, Conflict Management Skills for Women (videotape) (Mission, KS: SkillPath Publications, 1994).

• I need to take some time because I'm beginning to forget that you're the boss.

Use that one at your own risk! While it is clever, it can be taken as aggressive.

Be aware of two important points about using an exit line.

1. Always say when you will be back.
2. After you use the line, you need to LEAVE! Do not say it unless you mean it.

If they follow you and get pushy, say:

• Now is not a good time.

Repeat it several times if necessary. Make it clear that you do mean what you say. While you are in "time out," review your PowerPhrases and plan how to proceed.

Defusing Anger

Do not resist anger. Defuse it instead.

When you assert yourself by giving corrective feedback, a common first response is defensiveness. Expect and allow for that. Refrain from pushing them to acknowledge anything in that moment if they seem extremely upset.

Have you ever had someone spitting mad around you? Have you had someone who seemed out of control with anger? Do not resist their anger. Defuse it instead. If they are hurling accusations at you, avoid words like:

— *That is not true! (Makes them more certain that it is.)*

— *How dare you! (Accusatory.)*

— *Shut up! (Makes them want to talk all the more.)*

Avoid saying:

— *Calm down! (Invalidates their emotions.)*

— *Be reasonable! (Points out that they are not being reasonable, which inflames them more.)*

— *Can't you see how right I am? (Or anything that*

they will interpret this way.)

— *I do not have to put up with this! (They think you deserve it and are avoiding responsibility.)*

There are six main ways to defuse anger: (1) Listen, (2) Agree, (3) Ask Specific Questions to Focus Them, (4) Use Humor, (5) Stand Up to Them and (6) Go For a Solution.

PowerPhrases to the Rescue— Choose Words to Defuse Anger

In her book True Power[3], Linda Larsen gives a dramatic example of using PowerPhrases to defuse anger. She was abducted by an escaped convict and held at gunpoint for six hours! At one point her abductor took the gun, pointed it straight at her head, cocked the trigger, and asked her "Are you ready to die?" Linda's mind worked like a computer, searching for the response that would not provoke her agitated captor. Her response was:

- Well, I suppose if you wanted to kill me there is nothing I can do to stop you.

Her abductor asked, —"Why aren't you on the floor groveling for your life?" To which she replied:

- Because you have the power.

What she realized as those words came out of her mouth was that SHE was the one with the power. He was out of control and she was in control. That enabled her to choose responses that helped her to successfully escape. Her goal in that moment was to stay alive. To do that, she needed to align with her captor, not alienate him. Whatever your goals are, avoid unnecessarily provoking the other person. That will enhance your chances of success.

Whatever your goals are, avoid unnecessarily provoking the other person.

[3] Linda Larsen, *True Power*, Sarasota FL, Brandywine Publications, 2000.

1. Listening to Defuse Anger

Usually people who are angered expect you to resist. The very act of listening rather than resisting often defuses anger. When listening to an angry person you will need to use **PowerPhrases to Acknowledge Without Agreeing,** such as:

• I can see you feel strongly about this.

• I did not know you felt that way.

• Tell me more.

• What else concerns you?

Refer back to page 60 for more of these phrases.

Power Listening to the Rescue

Debbie had to fire one of her employees. Unfortunately, this employee's wife, Betty, was on Debbie's management team. Debbie noticed that Betty had become indirectly hostile so she invited Betty to discuss it. The discussion amounted to about twenty minutes of Debbie listening to Betty yell, during which Debbie used PowerPhrases to acknowledge her feelings and encourage Betty to speak. After expressing herself this way, Betty seemed relieved, and there was no more indirect aggression.

Months later, there was an opening for a position Debbie wanted in the department Betty oversaw. When Debbie expressed interest she got Betty's full support, and now is very happy in her new position.

Even though Debbie was quite justified in firing Betty's husband and the accusations that were hurled at her were unwarranted, it was in Debbie's interests to resist defending herself and to allow Betty to vent the anger she felt. Do not let your ego tell you to do things that are ultimately not in your best interest.

People who are angered expect you to resist. The very act of listening rather than resisting often defuses anger.

2. Using Agreement to Defuse Anger

Listen for something you can agree to. It may be that out of a hundred accusations, you can hear only one that has validity. Validate that point! As a skilled conflict manager, listen for truth in everything that is said. There is a good chance that the speaker does not know what the real issue is. Listen for the deeper truth, and help them sort out the issues and move forward into problem solving. A side benefit is that when you validate what truth you find, they often will calm down and be more open to listening.

Here are words to avoid:

— *Ninety-nine things you said are wrong.*

— *How can you think that?*

— *Aren't you ignoring the following 200 facts?*

Listen for truth in everything that is said.

Instead, use a **PowerPhrase to Defuse Anger by Agreeing,** such as:

• **The point you made about ___ hits home.**

• **That may be…**

• **I don't blame you for being upset about…**

• **I hate it when that happens to me too!**

• **I get angry too when…**

Align yourself with them and put yourself in the same boat. While they are attempting to make you the enemy, you see the similarities between you.

Power Thinking to the Rescue

Observe your thoughts when someone is venting anger at you. Some thoughts that will get you in trouble are:

— *I've got to stop them.*

— *They have their nerve.*

— *I can't handle this!*

Instead, use Power Thoughts, such as:

• Stay calm.

• What can I say to calm them down?

• What do they need in this moment?

• What is the issue behind their emotion?

• What might they be afraid of?

Choose thoughts that focus on your main goal at that moment—calming them down so that you can focus on the real issue. Do not get caught up in their emotion. You choose your own response.

Defuse anger by seeking specific information.

3. Ask Specific Questions to Defuse Anger

Often when people are angry, the accusations are sweeping. You always... you never... you are a such and such. Often they will label you. You can defuse the anger by seeking specific information to get them to focus on a concrete subject. This tool also keeps you from resisting the accusations.

You will probably have to put yourself on a leash to listen to accusations that are hurled at you in anger! In fact, you will want to deny the accusation even if you don't believe what they are accusing you of is so bad! When they are out of control in anger, this is not the time to say:

— *That's not true.*

— You're wrong.

— How dare you!

— Yeah but you...

Instead, use a **PowerPhrase for Diffusing Anger Through Inquiry,** such as:

- Exactly what do I say or do that leads you to believe that...

- You just said that ... (I lied, I am stupid, etc....) Will you explain what you mean by that?

- To really understand your point, I need specific examples.

This tool disarms, as well as forces them to get more logical rather than emotional.

4. Using Humor to Defuse Anger

The best humor pokes fun at the person using it.

Humor in explosive situations can backfire, so use these phrases with caution. You do not want to give the impression that you take their concerns lightly. Your goal is to break the angry state and introduce some levity. The best humor pokes fun at the person using it. Avoid humor at the expense of the angry person. Instead, use a **PowerPhrase to Defuse Anger With Humor,** such as:

- Someone must have switched stupid pills with my vitamins.

- You know, Brad Pitt was saying the exact same thing to me last week!

- I wonder if my mother dropped me on my head as a baby!

- Don't hurt me! I'm a grandmother!

- Is there a mess-up of the month award?

- My brain has a mind of its own sometimes.

If these do not sound like PowerPhrases to you, consider this: powerful people are confident enough that they do not need to constantly prove how great they are. In addition, PowerPhrases seek results. The result we seek when someone is out of control is to help him or her calm down so we can proceed to conflict management.

5. Stand Up to an Angry Person

If these PowerPhrases get you nowhere in a situation where someone seems emotionally out of control, you could be communicating with a manipulator or a tester. Some people become deliberately angry to control the listener. Others become deliberately angry to test the listener. Staying calm frustrates the manipulator, and shows them that you are not someone to manipulate. Staying calm proves your strength to the tester. If your attempts to defuse fail and if you believe that you are dealing with a tester or manipulator, speak up on your own behalf. Some words to avoid are:

— *You're manipulating me. (They probably don't realize it.)*

— *Shut up! (Inflames and sounds helpless.)*

Instead, use a **PowerPhrase to Tell an Angry Person How to Treat You,** such as:

- **I care about your problem and when you speak to me in this way, I cannot focus on solutions.**

- **I want to hear what you have to say, but not in this way.**

- **I am here to find resolution. I am not here to be verbally abused. One more comment like that and I will no longer listen.**

- **Are you aware that you are blasting the very person who can help you?**

The result we seek when someone is out of control is to help him or her calm down so we can proceed to conflict management.

- When you speak to me in this way, I do not feel moved to help you.
- I am concerned about your problem and uncomfortable with the way you are expressing it.
- Speaking to me in this way is totally unacceptable.
- When you are calm, I will be happy to listen to your concerns.

These phrases make it clear what you will and won't accept without adopting their behaviors.

6. Going for a Solution to Defuse Anger

Out of control people usually are not ready to talk about solutions until they have had a chance to vent their emotions and assign a bit of blame. Sometimes, however, they will allow you to redirect their attention from the problem on to a solution. Use a **PowerPhrase to Focus on the Solution,** such as:

- Let's fix the problem, instead of blame.
- What can I do for you now?
- How do you see us resolving this problem?

If they are out of control with anger, use these phrases with caution, as they might become angrier if they have a stronger need to emote than to find resolution.

Out of control people usually are not ready to talk about solutions until they have had a chance to vent their emotions and assign a bit of blame.

PowerPhrase to the Rescue— Defuse Anger by Seeking Solutions

My friend Susan was on a committee that changed the charting for the hospital she worked at. The first day the new charts came into effect, a doctor called and asked,

"Whose crazy idea was these new charts?"

Susan said:

- I was part of a committee that put these charts together.

The doctor said, "You nurses are ruining this hospital." To which Susan responded:

- Sir, there was a doctor on the committee.

The doctor responded to that by saying, "So now you're blaming the doctors!"

Susan decided that she needed to go for a solution. She said:

- With things being what they are, what can I do for you now?

He said "I want the following points documented and on my desk by Monday at ten."

If Susan had tried to show him how irrational his communication was, she would still be arguing with him. Going for a solution sidestepped the fixing of blame.

Defuse anger by seeking solutions.

PowerPhrases for Dealing With Passive-Aggressive Behavior

Do you find directly angry people easy to deal with compared to the ones who are indirect or passive-aggressive? Passive-aggressive people are out to get you, but they use indirect tactics. If you address the issue directly, they deny the problem, and act innocent.

Passive-aggression comes in four main forms.

1. Mixed messages. ("Not bad for a novice.")

2. Tone of voice conflicts with literal meaning of wording. ("So glad you could make it!" in a sarcastic tone that emphasizes the word "make.")

3. Gestures conflict with words. (Saying "of course" while rolling the eyes.)

4. Actions conflict with words. (Saying, "Let's do it your way!" but not following through.)

People are passive-aggressive for three reasons.

1. They do not know how to or do not feel safe with communicating directly.

2. They can get away with it.

3. They are unconscious of their actions.

In all cases, deal with passive-aggression in a straightforward way. Describe the conflict between what they are saying and what you perceive. Do not say:

— *You lie! (Accusatory)*

— *Oh yeah? Right! (Sarcastic and passive-aggressive)*

Instead, use a **PowerPhrase to Address Passive-Aggressive Behavior Directly,** such as:

- **Is something bothering you that we need to address? I care about our relationship. If there is something we need to resolve, let's do it.**

Passive-aggressive people are out to get you but they use indirect tactics.

- I am confused because your words say everything is fine, but your tone of voice implies it's not. What's going on?
- What do you mean by…?
- That remark sounded sarcastic and condescending to me. Did you mean it that way?
- When you say ___, this is what I hear… Is that what you mean?
- I thought I heard a dig. Did I?
- When you said ___, I heard___. That hurts!

Do not expect them to instantly confess their tactics! Passive-aggressive people will continue the tactics that have worked so well for them until they realize they do not work anymore. If they deny any truth to your perceptions, do not worry about it. If you stay assertive, over time they will stop.

Passive-aggressive people will continue their tactics until they realize they do not work anymore.

If they accuse you of being too sensitive, you do not need to automatically deny it. Avoid saying:

— No, I am not! (*Sounds defensive and you are playing their game, not yours.*)

You can simply respond by saying:

- That may be. If I am sensitive, I think it is important for you to know how your words affect me.
- If you believe I am sensitive, why do you make comments like that?
- This is not an issue of sensitivity. This is an issue of…

If they say it was just a joke, you can tell them:

- If you intended it as a joke, you need to know that I did not find it funny. Instead of being amused, I was hurt.
- Sometimes I use humor to mask put-downs or to communicate issues indirectly. If that is what you

are doing, and if there is something you need to tell me, please tell me directly.

Power Pointer— It Is Hard to See Passive-Aggressiveness in Ourselves.

Georgia was upset that people would criticize coworkers who were not in attendance at meetings. She took the meeting minutes, so one day she took the minutes verbatim. Every dig and every sideswipe went into the minutes. Georgia felt innocent and acted baffled that people were angry about it. Georgia had no idea that her action was passive aggressive. She was being indirectly hurtful. A more assertive approach would have been to say something like:

We always have options of assertiveness.

- I am uncomfortable when we speak about people behind their backs. I insist that we only talk about people in the same way we would if they were here.

Of course she would need to be willing to back up her assertion with action. If the behavior continued, she could assert herself again.

- When we criticize people who are not present, it causes me to wonder if you discuss me when I am not here. I find it unacceptable.

If there is still no response she can walk out of the meeting, asserting:

- Please invite me back when this discussion has ended.

Passive-aggressive behavior in ourselves is hard to see, because we believe that they deserve so much worse than what we are giving them. We always have options of assertiveness.

EXERCISE

I. Listening While Under Attack

Get a friend you feel very comfortable with for this exercise, because it will probably stretch your tolerance level! Ask your friend to hurl criticism and accusations at you. If you are really adventurous, tell them the areas you are sensitive about. For example, if being called selfish is a problem for you, tell your friend to call you selfish. If you are not so bold, ask them to limit themselves to specific comments that do not trigger such core issues.

When they make an accusation, respond by telling them what you appreciate about them. Your comments do not have to relate to their criticisms in any way. For example, they might call you selfish, and you respond by saying they have sound business judgment. They say you are stupid and you tell them that they have nice hair.

The purposes of this exercise it to break the pattern of reacting. It is very powerful.

II. Make Your CASE

Problem: Someone expressed your idea to the boss and took credit.

Your Response: You naturally believe you know what happened. The coworker you confided in is not to be trusted! She wronged you! However, do you really know the entire story? Instead of accusing her or getting back at her, you make your CASE! You start by clarifying her position.

What **PowerPhrases to Ask Clarifying Questions** would you use?

1._____

2._____

3._____

She says things that sound like excuses to you, but in order to stay focused on her perspective and to get the entire story, you use a **PowerPhrase to Acknowledge Without Agreeing**. Which ones do you use?

1._____

2._____

3._____

She begins by saying that it was as much her idea as yours. She says she never told the boss it was her idea, he just assumed that it was. She also expresses her own fear about being fired if she does not come up with some great ideas. You are ready to respond, but before you do, you want to verify your understanding by using a **PowerPhrase to Ask Questions That Confirm Understanding**. What do you say?

Now you know what to say because you understand her position. You want to make certain that she is ready to listen, and you want to set the stage for uninterrupted time. You do this by using a **PowerPhrase for Requesting to Express Yourself Without Interruption.** What do you say?

She agrees to hear you out. First, you want to describe the problem using a **PowerPhrase for Describing Negative Behavior.** How do you describe the problem in objective terms?

Now you want to communicate the impact the behavior had on you by using a **PowerPhrase for Expressing the Impact of a Behavior.** What do you say?

Next, express your suggested solutions by using a **PowerPhrase for Requesting a New Behavior.** What do you say?

Congratulations! You asserted your position! However, your coworker responds with sarcasm. She says, "I guess not everyone is as perfect as you are."

You respond by using a **PowerPhrase to Address Passive-Aggressive Behavior Directly.** What do you say?

Now she knows that you are calm and you are serious. You are ready to reach an agreement. Use a **PowerPhrase to Request That You Negotiate Solutions Together.** What do you say?

_____

_____

She agrees and you come up with several options. What options do you come up with? Be certain there is something to be gained for her as well as you.

_____

_____

_____

_____

Together you choose one option. This issue does not seem to call for written agreements or follow-up so you skip that step. Thank her for working with you, and decide how much information you feel safe sharing with her in the future.

www.scubaz.ca

Learn why *Reasonableness Is Your Best Revenge* at:
http://www.speakstrong.com/articles/speak-strong/reasonableness.html

POWERPHRASES®

CHAPTER 5

PowerPhrases® for Negotiations to Get You What You Want

Look at the following and say aloud what you see.
OPPORTUNITYNOWHERE
If you saw:
OPPORTUNITY NOWHERE,
you are not alone. If you saw:
OPPORTUNITY NOW HERE,
great job! Your focus was positive!

Your success with negotiations starts with picturing a positive outcome. Jim Cathcart said, "The hardest part about getting where I am today was picturing myself being where I am today."[4] Similarly, the hardest part about having a successful negotiation is in being able to picture the possibility. The second hardest part is to know what to say. That's where PowerPhrases are so handy! PowerPhrases will serve you from pre-negotiation to post-negotiation.

The hardest part about having a successful negotiation is in being able to picture the possibility.

Pre-negotiation Essentials
Research Before Beginning to Negotiate

Most of your work in a negotiation takes place before you sit at the negotiation table. Doing your homework can take time, but it is time invested, not spent. PowerPhrases can help.

[4] Jim Cathcart, *The Pros Speak About Success,* (Mission KS: SkillPath Publications, 1999)

Before you embark on your negotiation, find out:

1. What are the standards in the area, and what is a reasonable range?

2. What do you want and what are you willing to accept?

3. What are they likely to want and why?

4. What are your deadlines as well as theirs?

5. What are their options if you cannot come to agreement and what alternatives do you have? (This is called walk-away power.)

As part of your research, talk to:

1. People who have already negotiated with the person or organization you will be negotiating with.

2. People who work with the person or team you will be negotiating with. For example, the design department can provide you with useful information about the sales department.

3. Neighbors or neighboring business people.

4. The person you will be negotiating with.

Doing your homework can take time, but it is time invested, not spent. PowerPhrases can help.

PowerPhrases provide the words to get the information you need. When researching with outside parties, use **PowerPhrases to Get Information About the Other Person's Situation,** such as:

• **What pressures are they under?**

• **What deadlines are they under?**

• **What is the mood in the organization right now?**

• **What kind of arrangements have they made with others either currently or in the past?**

• **If I offered _____, would I be in the ballpark?**

• **What alternatives do they have to making a deal with me?**

• **How willing are they to take a risk in this matter?**

• **To whom does the negotiator answer?**

- Why do they want what they do? What need are they trying to meet?
- How flexible are they?
- How do they decide…?

Adapt these phrases when your research involves speaking with the actual party you will be negotiating with.

Prepare yourself as much as you can before you actually begin a negotiation. While you certainly will be uncovering information in the actual negotiations process, get as much information as you can before you approach the table.

Set the Tone

Once you believe you have learned all you can, initiate the negotiation in a way that creates an atmosphere of confidence, ease and mutual gain. Use words that suggest benefit to the other person. You may choose to avoid the word "negotiate," which can imply a winner and a loser. Avoid saying:

> — Let's negotiate.

> — I'll do whatever it takes to win your business.

> — I'll have you seeing things my way in no time.

Initiate the negotiation in a way that creates an atmosphere of confidence, ease and mutual gain.

Instead, use a **PowerPhrase to Initiate a Negotiation,** such as:

- If we could work out a plan that benefits us both, would you be interested?
- Let's come to an agreement on this.
- Let's work together to find a plan that works for both of us.
- I am here to work with you.
- Let's discuss the situation and come up with a solution we both are happy with. I do not want either of us to agree to anything that does not

satisfy both our needs.

- We have a challenge. Let's find a solution together.
- I'm convinced that we can find an agreement that we both like.
- I have an idea I want to share with you. I need 15 minutes of your undivided attention. Would 3:00 this afternoon work?

Power Pointer— Set the Tone Immediately

I was called in to assist a national company with management-employee negotiations. The manager who introduced me was light and playful with the group until we were ready to begin. At that point he introduced me by telling the group how serious things were and warning them of how they needed to listen, not interrupt, do what I said and shape up. He sounded condescending and patronizing. Everyone's faces fell as a me-against-you atmosphere was created. I knew that if I was going to win any trust from the employees, I needed to change that perception fast. I also needed to avoid offending the manager who had called me in. I said:

- Michael is right. This is a serious situation and it does need to be taken seriously. Because it is so serious, let's relax and have as much fun as we can as we go about resolving the issues that face us today. Serious solutions to serious issues come from a state of openness and relaxation. That is when we are our most creative, and that is how we will find answers that satisfy both sides here.

The tone changed back to one of lightness, cooperativeness and one where solutions could be uncovered.

If the tone of a negotiation is not favorable for solutions, focus on lightening the tone before you dive into the negotiation details.

If the tone of a negotiation is not favorable for solutions, focus on lightening the tone before you dive into the negotiation details.

To help create a relaxed attitude, personalize the conversation. Use their name, and make it a conversation between two people, not two positions. Avoid saying:

— *ABC Widgets has a proposal they would like to make to XYZ Whatis.*

Instead, use a **PowerPhrase to Personalize the Negotiation,** such as:

- Kathy, I would like to discuss the deal I can offer you.

- Bill, sit down and get comfortable before we begin.

- Matt, I believe we have a lot to offer each other.

- Janet, I can tell that you are very experienced in this area.

Determine Authority

Always be certain that you are negotiating with the person who has the authority to make a deal. You can find that out with **PowerPhrases to Find the Decision Maker,** such as:

- Who else would you need to consult before we can come to final terms?

- If we reach an agreement, will anyone else have to approve?

- How does it work around here? Is this a decision you can make?

- If we reach an agreement today, can we move ahead?

- If we came to an agreement here today, what would your next step be?

- If we strike a deal, can you approve it?

- Is there someone else involved in this agreement with you?

- If you are happy with what we conclude here, when can we get started?

To help to create a relaxed attitude, personalize the conversation.

If someone else does need to be consulted, either say:

- **I am unwilling to negotiate without the decision maker present.**

Or say:

- **I would be happy to sit in on meetings with the final decision maker to provide backup information.**

Be aware that if the person you are negotiating with is not the final authority, you might give them enough information to be convinced themselves, but not enough for them to convince someone else. Also, many times when a deal is submitted to a "higher authority" for approval, they are using a tactic to come back with a better deal for them.

Many times when a deal is submitted to a "higher authority" for approval, they are using a tactic to come back with a better deal for them.

Graciously Asking Probing Questions

Once the tone is set, you are negotiating with the right person, and you are ready to begin discussing issues, put the initial focus on them and their needs.

Use a **PowerPhrase to Solicit Their Position**, such as:

- **What goals do you have for today?**

- **How would you like to see this discussion turn out?**

- **Is there anything you want me to know?**

- **What do you see as our common ground here?**

- **Tell me what you want from me/us.**

- **I want to make certain this turns out in a way that works for everybody. How do you see that happening?**

- **How will you know...(which supplier you want)?**

Listen, listen, and listen to what they have to say. You will do your best negotiating when you do far more listening than talking! Ask clarifying questions, acknowledge without agreeing, and learn everything that you can.

Use a **PowerPhrase** to **Ask Clarifying Questions in Negotiations**, such as:

- Could you expand on that?
- Please give me more details about…
- I need more precise information about that last point.
- Is there anything else we need to discuss that would add significant cost to us?
- Have I summarized everything?

Paraphrase their offers back to them, using a **PowerPhrase to Clarify Understanding**, such as:

- Am I correct in understanding that…?
- I think I understand what you are saying, but I want to be certain I know just what you mean. Are you saying that…?
- What I understand you to be saying is…
- Let me check to see if I understand you correctly. Are you saying that…?

Be certain your understanding of their position is accurate before you assert your own.

You will do your best negotiating when you do far more listening than talking!

Power Pointer—The Importance of Acknowledgement

When I coach people during negotiations, I always look for the areas where the parties are in need of acknowledgement. In one discussion, Joe was pointing out to Susan the ways in which she was not giving as much as he expected of her. Susan became defensive and insisted that she was bending over backwards to meet his expectations. Susan was unable to hear how she was falling short because she was seeking acknowledgement of the effort she was putting forward. Joe was unwilling to acknowledge her efforts because he expected more. He was concerned that if he acknowledged her, she would not continue to improve. This is a common impasse. When I was able to get them to see the nature of their stalemate they both relented and were able to give the other the needed acknowledgement and move on. Many times, an unmet need for acknowledgement is the greatest obstacle to finding solutions. People want to get credit for whatever they give.

Maintaining Early Neutrality

Do you ever have an emotional reaction to the other person's offer? No matter how unreasonable or exciting their offer seems to you in the beginning, maintain a sense of neutrality early in the negotiation. Get a complete picture before you respond to the pieces. Your previous homework of determining standards and alternatives will give you power in responding to their offers. If you do not have attractive options or if their initial offer is very reasonable, you might be tempted to show enthusiasm that could weaken the possibilities of getting concessions. Even if you feel your very survival depends on working out a deal, avoid saying:

— I've got to have this or I'll die!

— This is exactly what I've been looking for!

— That's a terrific buy!

— You are our only supplier.

Instead, use a **PowerPhrase to Sound Calm in Negotiation,** such as:

• I think we might be able to work out a deal.

• What you have could work for me.

• Let's talk specifics and see if there is a way we can make this work.

Early neutrality keeps your options open.

Making Your Offer

When you are ready to make an offer, state your needs and offers clearly and confidently. Avoid:

— I really don't like asking you to do this but...

— I was hoping that maybe you possibly could...

— You probably won't want to, but...

Use a **PowerPhrase for Making an Offer,** such as:

• I propose that...

• In my view, a fair solution would be...

• I strongly recommend that...

• One solution that I see working for us both is...

• One fair arrangement would be...

• If we do ____, it would benefit you by___.

Use specific amounts. Don't say:

— I'll give you around $3000.

Early neutrality keeps your options open.

Instead, use a **PowerPhrase for Stating a Specific Amount or Commitment**, such as:

• I am prepared to offer $2973.

• I will have this completed by June 13 at 3:30 PM.

The other party is less likely to argue with a specific amount or deadline. State your needs clearly. Without being frivolous, ask for what you really want, not just what you think you can get.

• What I want is___. What this would mean to you is___.

• What I want is___ by ___ because___.

Then show how you are able to fill their needs. Be sure to emphasize why it is a great deal for them.

Use **PowerPhrases to Communicate Value to Them**, such as:

• What this means for you is...

• I can help you by...

• Obviously ____ is important to you. I can help you with...

• One of the advantages I/we offer is...

The other party will be less likely to argue with a specific amount or deadline.

Power Thinking to the Rescue— Starting High Can Benefit Them as Well as You

When you ask for what you really want rather than being limited by what you think you can get, you are much more likely to end up better off. If your initial position is high but not frivolous, they have more room to talk you down and still give you a good deal. Imagine your initial offer is $15, but you come down to $10. They can go back to their boss and say they got you down 33%!

Now, imagine you start at $12, and go down to $9. When they report the results they do not look as good, even though the price is more favorable!

Watch out for thoughts like:

— *They might think I'm trying to take advantage of them.*

— *They might get upset if I ask for what I really want.*

Instead, think:

• The worst that can happen is that they will say no.

• This is what I want and this is what it's worth, so this is what I will ask for.

• I need to create some room for them to work with.

Early neutrality keeps your options open.

If you have areas of weakness, minimize the impact by addressing them directly.

Use a **PowerPhrase to Minimize Weakness**, such as:

- **Although we do not have the experience you normally require, what we do offer is...**

- **What we offer instead of...is...**

- **It is true that ___ is not our strong point; however, it is a minor issue in this discussion.**

Then move on to emphasize the parts of the deal that they like.

Get feedback from them regarding your offer by using a **PowerPhrase to Solicit Feedback for Your Offers**, such as:

- **What do you think of this idea?**

- **Do you have any concerns with this proposal?**

- **What do you like about my offer?**

If their expectations are unrealistic, let them know without offending. Avoid saying:

— *It's not fair.*

— *You're way off base.*

Instead, use a **PowerPhrase to Suggest the Range**, such as:

- **That offer is not competitive.**

- **I cannot come close to that.**

- **Those expectations are unrealistic.**

- **My budget is not close to your range.**

If they do not respond immediately, remain silent until they do.

If you have areas of weakness, minimize the impact by addressing them directly.

Give and Take in Negotiations

If their initial offer is ridiculously low or ridiculously high, steer clear of the following Poison Phrases:

— *Oh no! This is going to cost me more than I thought!*

— *You're crazy!*

— *That's highway robbery!*

— *What is your problem?*

— *I disagree.*

Instead, consider not countering. Be prepared with **PowerPhrase Responses to Their Offers.** Say:

• That's an interesting offer.

• Let's get serious.

• I'm confused. (Silence)

• I can begin to negotiate seriously with you when you recommend ideas that are reasonable.

• I believe you want to be fair with me, but this offer is not reasonable.

• That offer tells me that you are not serious about coming to an agreement. Am I right?

Alternatively, you can counter with your own extreme offer.

• If that is your initial offer, my initial offer will be as extreme in the other direction.

If their initial offer is ridiculously low or ridiculously high, consider not countering.

Consider countering an extreme offer with a counter proposal that is equally extreme.

Power Pointer— Life IS a Negotiation

When Sandy began negotiations for a divorce settlement, she did not realize that she was in a negotiation. She suggested settlements that seemed fair to her. Her husband was playing the negotiation game in a very different way. He began with an extreme position that was in many ways unreasonable.

Because Sandy did not consider this to be a negotiation, she was not prepared for her husband's approach. As a result, her very fair position became the starting point for her position in the negotiation. Her husband was pushing her toward a final settlement that was a middle ground between her position and his extreme position–an outcome that favored him.

When Sandy woke up to what was really going on, she began to push for concessions she never believed she could get. She was shocked when her husband responded by relenting on other things that she did not expect.

If you limit yourself to what you think you can get, you relinquish much of your power.

Be aware of the other party's attitude. Be aware that some negotiators do not respect soft negotiators and actually prefer to work with people who pursue stronger positions. They enjoy the game, as well as the sense of victory that comes with overcoming some of the demands of a tough "opponent."

Or you can ask:

• Where did you get that figure?

• What caused you to decide on that...(price, deadline, specification)?

• If you were in my seat would you consider that a serious offer?

Power Pointer— Speaking Powerfully Can Take Getting Used To!

One of my clients was very uncomfortable after reading this book. Fred was in the middle of a negotiation to sell a business. Fred's habit was to give in, go along with what the other person wanted, and "jump through hoops" to meet someone else's demands. The only alternative he saw was to be combative. Fred wanted to respond in a different way and the idea frightened him.

We found the middle ground of being open, firm and committed to a fair deal. We worked out the PowerPhrases to back him up in his new stance.

Fred found that having the words gave him the courage to be his own advocate. The words did not eliminate his fear, however. Despite his fear he was able to stand his ground and speaking was easier for him the next time. Do not wait for the fear to go away. Be prepared with your PowerPhrases, and forge ahead!

Do not wait for the fear to go away. Take action anyway.

Even when offers are within range or better than you imagined, consider going after a sweeter deal, if only to make them feel good about the deal they make. When you accept an offer too quickly, they will think that they went too cheap. If it is a reasonable offer, affirm that with a **PowerPhrase to Express Partial Disagreement,** such as:

• Your offer is reasonable for the most part. There are some areas that concern me...

• While I agree on the whole, I have trouble agreeing with the point about...

You can counter their offer by using a **PowerPhrase to Counter an Offer**, such as:

• I can offer you ___, if you can give me___.

• I understand you feel your price is justified. However, I can only pay...

• I need... because...

• That's not what I had in mind.

• I need you to do better than that.

• The best I can do is...

• Is that the best you can do?

• What is your bottom line?

• What would it take to get you to raise (lower) your price?

• What if we changed (specifications) (deadline) (the price)?

• I was thinking more along the lines of ...

• Would you consider...?

• What would you say to...?

• Let's brainstorm options together.

Next, start the brainstorming process.

Even when you like an offer, it can benefit you to make a counter offer.

Brainstorming

You have an infinite number of possible ways to design a deal. Use brainstorming to generate as many ideas as possible in order to come up with creative solutions. Start by thinking of as many ideas as you can without worrying about why any of them will not work.

When you want to brainstorm with the other person, use

a PowerPhrase to Initiate the Brainstorming Process, such as:

- I've run out of ideas. How do you think we can resolve this?
- What do you REALLY want?
- What's the craziest solution you can think of to this problem?
- How can we expand on the ideas we already have on the table?
- Suppose we were to...
- What if...
- Let's assume...

When you brainstorm, remember that there are no bad or ridiculous ideas. A "crazy idea" can lead to a great one. Evaluate ideas separately from creating them.

If some of the ideas are negative, translate them into positives. If you consider suggesting:

> — I can refuse to fill orders that are under 30 days.

Say:

- I can fill orders that are over 30 days.

Suspend judgment while you brainstorm, and evaluate these ideas later.

You have an infinite number of possible ways to design a deal.

Brainstorming together works best when the trust level is high. The best deals are made when you both are helping each other meet goals. Of course, ultimately you both will be loyal to your self or organization. Be alert for objections and tactics.

Dealing With Objections and Tactics

Be prepared for objections and tactics as well as the objections that are used as tactics. When they state an objection, use a **PowerPhrase to Overcome Objections,** such as:

• I understand how you feel. Many others have felt the same way. What they found was ___.

• Are you saying that if I can satisfy this objection, we would have a deal?

• Is that the only barrier between you and an agreement?

• It's because I know that you are concerned with (their objection) that I think this is a fabulous offer for you.

• What makes you say that?

• What's keeping you from getting the best?

Need to Think About It

If they say that they need to think about it, respectfully offer to be a part of their thinking process, so that they won't talk themselves out of it due to lack of understanding.

If they they need to think about it, offer to be a part of their thinking process.

Use a **PowerPhrase to Counter Their Need to Think About It,** such as:

• What questions remain?

• Could you think about it out loud?

• I can help you to think about it if you will tell me what your concerns are.

Sometimes the need to think about an offer is legitimate, so it's important not to push. Offer your support as a service to them in helping to clarify their concerns.

Split the Difference

If they want to split the difference between their position and yours, and they are within your range, use a **PowerPhrase to Raise the Range,** such as:

• I'm at (ten) and you're at (six). Are you suggesting that you could come up to (eight)? Let me discuss that with my people and let you know.

The range is now between eight and ten. This makes nine seem reasonable.

If they want to split the difference and they are out of range, make value the criteria.

Use a **PowerPhrase to Focus the Discussion on Value**, such as:

- **You are offering me ___. What standard did you use to get that amount?**
- **I would gladly split the difference if I thought that doing so would result in a fair amount. In this case I do not find it reasonable.**

Splitting the difference can be an attempt to frame the figures in a way that might not be relevant.

Nibblers

Never make a concession without receiving something of value in return. If they are "nibbling"–meaning that they are asking for many seemingly insignificant concessions–and the concessions are adding up, use a **PowerPhrase to End Nibbling Negotiators**, such as:

- **If I do that for you, what will you do for me?**
- **If you have to have that, I have to have this.**

Even if what you ask for is relatively insignificant, it makes it clear that you are setting boundaries.

Good Guy–Bad Guy

If you haven't run into the good guy–bad guy game, you have at least seen it on television. This is a ploy used when you are negotiating with a team. One negotiator is positioned as being "on your side" and the other is positioned as the "bad" one. The "good" one tries to convince you to trust them to help you to deal with the "unreasonable" one. When this happens, challenge them on the tactic.

Never make a concession without receiving something of value in return.

111

Use a **PowerPhrase to Challenge the Good Guy–Bad Guy Game**, such as:

- You aren't going to play good guy/bad guy with me, are you?

- I think ___ is playing bad guy, but let's not approach it that way. Let's take the win-win approach.

Deal with indirect behavior in negotiations the same way you do in conflict. Let them know you see through their game.

Bogey

A bogey is when the other person claims to be powerless due to a limited budget, deadlines, quality standards, etcetera. Test it out.

Use a **PowerPhrase to Test a Constraint**, such as:

Deal with indirect behavior in negotiations directly.

- If I found the perfect item for (20%) more, should I bother showing it to you?

- Who has the authority to (exceed the budget, change the deadline, alter specifications)?

- Have there been situations where you have exceeded the budget? How can we make this situation like that one?

Use these PowerPhrases to find the limits to their stated constraints.

Use Some Tactics of Your Own

A. Higher Authority

You can try to get a more favorable agreement by referring to a higher authority. If they ask for a concession you do not wish to give, use a **PowerPhrase to Defer to a Higher Authority**, such as:

- I can agree to x, but beyond that I will have to consult my general manager, who is out of town for the

next two weeks.
- Our policy is...
- I can't sell this to my manager.

Many times they will concede rather than wait.

B. Last Minute Concessions

You also can ask for some last minute concessions by using a **PowerPhrase for Extracting Last Minute Concessions,** such as:

- You've got a deal if you will...
- I'll do it if you'll...

Often at that point they are so ready to firm up the deal that they will give away new concessions.

Know When and How to Walk Away

If you are willing to walk away from a deal, that willingness gives you power. If you discover and create options before beginning the negotiation, you will not settle for less than you deserve.

If you are willing to walk away from a deal, that willingness gives you power.

When you tell them you are ready to walk away, don't say:

— *Take it or leave it.*

— *Accept my offer or I'm outta here.*

Instead, use a **PowerPhrase for Rejecting an Offer,** such as:

- I find your offer unacceptable.

- No, your offer does not work for me.

- If that is the best you can do, we might as well not waste any more of each other's time.

- Perhaps we will be able to find mutually acceptable terms in future negotiations.

Do not give an ultimatum unless you are serious about it.

Sealing the Deal

When things are lining up the way you like them, be sure to confirm the deal before parting. Avoid saying:

— *Think about it and get back to me.*

— *You don't want this, do you?*

Or anything else that leaves the contract uncertain.

Instead, use a **PowerPhrase to Ask for an Agreement,** such as:

- This makes sense. Let's go ahead and make it happen.
- When shall we start?
- I believe we have a fair solution. Let's get the paperwork started and have it ready by ___.
- What will it take to get a commitment from you now?
- Let's put that in writing.

Be sure to confirm the deal.

Power Pointer— Get It in Writing!

I was coaching Bill through the sale of a franchise. He had sold it three years prior, and the man who bought it walked out on the business and turned it back to Bill without any notice. The last thing Bill wanted to do was come out of retirement, so he was very anxious to find a buyer.

He was lucky to find a buyer very quickly, and they worked as a team to keep the business going while negotiation details were being handled. The ownership of the franchise was transferred, they worked furiously to build up the inventory, and it looked like a smooth transition.

Bill was very happy about the feeling of good will in how it all unfolded, and because he had known the buyer for years, he was comfortable with acting on a verbal agreement of terms and the understanding that they would use the previous buyer's contract. Despite my misgivings, he was not in a hurry to get the contract in writing. He was very shocked when he received the contract. It included a clause that said "if payments are made on time for nine years, the tenth year is forgiven." That amounted to a 10% reduction in fee.

At this point he had lost all negotiation power and ended up agreeing to a deal that he did not like.

No matter how good it all feels, get your agreement in writing as soon as you can.

No matter how good it all feels, get it in writing as soon as you can.

If you cannot get them to commit on the spot, get them to commit to your next communication. Rather than leaving the discussion open, use a **PowerPhrase to Assure a Follow-Up Commitment**, such as:

• **When will you have your decision? Let's meet that day at ___ and wrap this up.**

If they say they will call you, ask when you can expect to hear from them. Once they have told you, use a **PowerPhrase for Maintaining Control of the Follow-Up,** such as:

• **If I haven't heard from you by ___ I will call you.**

Confirming the Agreement

Always be sure to acknowledge the other person for having made a good deal. Avoid saying:

— *I scored!*

— *If you were a better negotiator, you could have gotten more. (It happens!)*

Instead, use a **PowerPhrase for Acknowledging Their Decision**, such as:

• **You will be delighted with...**

• **I believe you did well for yourself.**

• **You are obviously skilled at negotiating.**

Now celebrate the fact that YOU are skilled at negotiating!

Always be sure to acknowledge them for having made a good deal.

EXERCISE

Imagine you want your boss to purchase a new piece of equipment for you, such as a printer or copy machine. What information do you want to obtain before initiating the negotiation?

_____

_____

_____

Some of this information will be obtained from other people. What PowerPhrases will you use to request it?

_____

_____

_____

Before you address the issue with your boss, you need to be clear about what you want and why. List your position (what you are asking for) below, followed by your reason for wanting what you do.

Your position:

_____

_____

_____

Reason for wanting what you do:

_____

_____

_____

What do you anticipate your boss's position will be, and why?

Boss's position:

_____

_____

_____

Reason for boss's position:

_____

_____

Let's say you want this piece of equipment because you are frustrated by the inconvenience of using group equipment. However, you present your desire in terms of the benefit to the boss. What PowerPhrases do you use?

_____

_____

The boss says she will review your recommendations and get back to you. What PowerPhrases will you use to maintain control of the follow-up?

_____

_____

_____

Quiz

When is most of the work done in a negotiation?

_____

What PowerPhrases can you use at that stage?

_____

_____

What do you have when you take the "n" off of negotiation?

_____

Which PowerPhrases address the ego of the other party in negotiation?

_____

_____

In a negotiation, who is likely to be the most persuasive—the one who talks the most, or the one who talks the least?

_____

_____

Exercise

Tape record a conversation when you are talking to a friend about something that they know a lot about and you know very little and you want to learn more. Play it back and evaluate who spoke the most.

Next record yourself trying to persuade them of something. Play it back and see who did the most talking.

If you were being truly persuasive, you would have done as little talking and as much listening as you did in the first part of the exercise. In order to be truly persuasive, ask questions and listen! PowerPhrases say it in as few words as possible. That gives you lots of time to listen!

Read *Ten Tips to SpeakStrong at a Trade Show*
http://www.speakstrong.com/articles/sales/tradeshowtips.html

CHAPTER 6:

PowerPhrases® That Sell

Selling… negotiating… what is the difference? Selling creates acceptance of an idea, and negotiating spells out the terms. Certainly the two concepts do overlap. Yet, there is enough difference that I am making the chapters separate.

Although this chapter is geared toward the professional sales person, if you do not have sales as part of your title, please study this chapter anyway! The PowerPhrases in this chapter will enable you to be more persuasive in life no matter what your focus is. Use the **PowerPhrases for Getting an Appointment** to get your boss to discuss your latest inspiration. Use the **PowerPhrases to Determine Needs** to find out whether the mechanic would be open to accepting frequent-flier miles instead of cash. Use the **PowerPhrases to Create Value** to show your boss that it would benefit her for you to get a copy machine of your own. Use the **PowerPhrases for Obtaining Commitment** to extract a promise from your spouse to take you to Hawaii. Just as we are all constantly negotiating, we are all constantly selling things and ideas. We might as well master the PowerPhrases to do it effectively.

Selling creates acceptance of an idea, and negotiating spells out the terms.

Know Your Objectives at Every Point of the Sale

Remember that PowerPhrases are clear about the results

they want to obtain with each expression. At different stages, you will have significantly different goals. When you are seeking an appointment, you must remember that your goal at that time is to get the appointment, NOT to close the sale. When you are investigating the needs of the prospect, your goal at that time is to discover the needs of the prospect; it is NOT to close the sale at that time. The PowerPhrases are specific to the immediate goal they serve.

Getting the Appointment in Cold Calls

The first step in getting an appointment is to get the attention of the prospect. The technique is simple!

Use the strongest **PowerPhrase to Get a Prospect's Attention** that exists. Call them by their name.

PowerPhrases are specific to the immediate goal they serve.

• Hello, Mr./Mrs./Ms. ____.

Then identify yourself.

• This is ___ from ___.

Next, briefly describe the purpose of your call. One approach would be to use a **PowerPhrase to Create Interest in What You Are Selling**, such as:

• If you believed that I could help you to meet your goals, you would want to hear about it, wouldn't you?

• I'm calling to show you a better way of doing business.

• Have you considered that your business could benefit from using ___?

• I can show you how you can add to your business by___.

• In x minutes, I can show you how our product can save your business $___. Can you give me those minutes?

- In a few minutes I can show you how to increase your bottom line by ___.
- I have something your company needs.
- How important is it to increase your bottom line?
- I represent a product that will make your life easier.

Another approach is to use a **PowerPhrase to Allude to a Referral**, such as:

- ___ suggested I call you. I have done a lot of work for her, and she suggested we might be of service to you.
- I'm calling because ___, who has been a client of mine since ___, is delighted with the results and felt certain that you would want to consider what we offer. Was he right?

Next you want to get a dialogue going by using a **PowerPhrase to Open a Discussion by Asking Questions They Can Answer Yes To**, such as:

- Is saving money important to you?
- Would you like to know how to increase motivation in your staff?
- Could you use an extra hour in the day?
- Does increased productivity interest you?
- We've been helping companies like yours prosper in today's marketplace. Would you like to know how?
- Do you ever get the sense that things take much longer than they should?

When you ask questions they can say yes to, you get them in a "yes" thinking style.

When you ask questions they can say yes to, you get them in a "yes" thinking style. Remember, at this point your goal is to get an appointment where you can provide them with complete information. Get them saying yes, and when you request the appointment, they will already be on a yes track. Explain how you can address their problem, but give only enough information to sell the appointment. Then ask for the appointment clearly. Avoid saying:

— *Could we meet?*

— *Can you fit me in sometime?*

— *I'll be in the neighborhood anyway next week and I'd like to stop by.*

Instead, use a **PowerPhrase to Get an Appointment**, such as:

- **Let's meet and discuss this in detail. Does Tuesday at 3:00 work for you?**

- **I suggest we talk in person Wednesday at 2:45. Can we plan on that?**

- **It will be more efficient and save us time if we talk face to face. I suggest we meet this Friday at 1:00.**

- **Can you free up 15 minutes to meet with me on Monday, or would Tuesday be better?**

- **Let me come by to explore and explain exactly what I can do for you.**

Sometimes getting the appointment will be that simple and sometimes it won't. When they offer an objection, repeat the objection back to them.

Follow with a **PowerPhrase to Overcome Their Objections to Meeting With You**. If they say they are too busy, say:

- **Is it as hectic there as it is here? I'm busy too, and that is why I do not want to waste either of our time. I am convinced that the time will be well spent.**

- **I had someone else tell me that just a few days ago. After meeting with me for 15 minutes, she was glad she made the time. May I tell you what she discovered while meeting with me?**

- **Is having too much to do with too little time your**

When they offer an objection, repeat the objection back to them.

biggest challenge right now? I can reclaim hours each week for you.

- My goal is to eliminate your time pressures with what my product offers.
- Can you find a few minutes to learn how to save time?
- That's exactly why we should get together!
- That's why I work very hard at making my presentation as brief as possible.

Power Pointer— Be Pleasantly Persistent.

It is a trick to know the difference between persistence and being pushy. Have you ever had someone overcome your resistance to meeting with him or her and been glad they did? The difference is usually in whether the salesperson is service oriented or not. Before you persist, ask yourself--"Do I believe that it is in THEIR interest to meet with me?" If the answer is yes, then proceed with confidence that you are serving their interest.

Most sales happen after the fifth attempt!

If they request literature, say:

- I don't send out literature. However, I can do better than that. I can meet with you personally...
- It would take you longer to read any information I could send you than it would for me to explain it. If time is important, let's meet face to face.

If they say they are not interested, do you immediately back down and give up? Most sales happen after the fifth attempt! Most people quit after the first attempt. Ten percent of sales people ask five times and get eighty percent of the yeses. You may decide that this person is not a true prospect, but if you believe that they need what you have to offer, keep asking. Say:

- Many of my loyal customers initially say just that, until they understand the nature of the product I represent.
- Really? You are concerned with the well-being of the company, aren't you?
- Do you mind telling me what you are interested in? Saving money? Improving morale?
- I must not have communicated what I offer very well, because I believe if I did, you would be interested.
- I don't expect that you would be interested until you saw how my service can improve performance.
- That surprises me. Can you explain why?
- You must have a good reason to say that. Can you explain it to me please?

If you believe that they need what you have to offer, keep asking.

If you believe that they are a true prospect, keep referring back to the **PowerPhrases to Get an Appointment** until you are convinced that this is a dead end or you have an appointment.

Establishing Wants and Needs at the Appointment

A. Situation Questions

While you will probe somewhat during the initial call to uncover wants and needs, most of this takes place face to face. Do not make the mistake of many sales professionals who move too quickly from the exploration stage into describing features and benefits of what they offer. People need to become aware of their problem and to feel the extent of its impact before they have much interest in hearing how you can solve that problem.

While you will want to get background information about the company from your prospect, questions that can be answered through preparatory research will not impress anyone, and those questions are not PowerPhrases. Do not sound like an interviewer. Questions like:

— *What do you produce?*

— *What are they composed of?*

— *How long have you been in business?*

— *How many people work here?*

are questions that you could research elsewhere. Particularly, do not ask questions that are unrelated to what the buyer is saying. Tie questions into what the buyer is saying and what the buyer's concerns are.

Use a **PowerPhrase to Determine the Situation of the Buyer,** such as:

• **Many of our customers have been affected by ___. How has that impacted you?**

• **How are you responding to (the recent change in market regulations)?**

• **How did you decide (to purchase the system that you are using now)?**

Consider your sales presentation as prime real estate. Whatever you build there must pay for itself in added value. Situation questions are PowerPhrases only when the information cannot be obtained prior to the sales interview.

B. Questions to Uncover Problems

Your questions about their concerns and difficulties will give you more value than situation questions. Ask questions about the challenges their situation creates.

Use **PowerPhrases to Uncover Problems,** such as:

• **Is (turnover) a problem here?**

• **Do (delayed deliveries) ever cost you business?**

Questions that can be answered through preparatory research will not impress anyone.

- What challenges do you have with (quality control)?
- How often are (deliveries delayed)?
- Is there an area where (quality control) could be improved?
- How satisfied are you with (your current supplier)?
- Are you concerned about (upcoming technology changes)?
- Where does (the process tend to break down)?
- It sounds like you're concerned about (high turnover). What can you tell me about that?
- Are you worried about...?
- What difficulties have you had with...?
- How are you handling...?

Ask questions about the challenges their situation creates.

Use these questions to find out where they hurt... and how you can help.

C. Questions to Clarify Problems

Get more information by responding to their concerns with in-depth questions to expand on their problems.

Use **PowerPhrases to Clarify Problems,** such as:

- Why is that a problem?
- What about that worries you?
- What is it about ___ that you are not satisfied with?
- Are you having any other difficulties with...?
- Tell me more about your problems with...

Clarification of the problem leads you to the next step, which is to ask questions about the implications of the problems they are describing. Use implication questions to uncover why the problem is important to the buyer. This gives you more information, and it also makes the buyer more aware of the need.

Use **PowerPhrases** to Reveal Implications of Problems, such as:

- How do those problems impact other departments?
- So does that mean that you...?
- Has that affected...?
- What is the impact of that problem on...?
- Has that led you to...?
- What is the result of that?

Buyers need to become aware of every area that is affected by the problem.

Use questions to find out where they hurt... and how you can help.

Sales professionals uncover and satisfy needs.

PowerPhrases in Unlikely Places

During a recent chat, an old friend mentioned his multimillion-dollar home and his swimming pool. Since it was hot and I wanted to keep up, I decided to invest in a pool of my own. I wanted one that fit my budget and tolerance for maintenance, so I took my business to KB Toys.

I went in looking for a small blow-up pool, and walked out with a large blow-up pool, a pool cover, a pump and an array of pool toys.

After asking me about where I live and what I wanted it for, the sales professional (yes, he was a professional!) said:

- Most people are much happier with the 5'x10' pool. They like the fact that you can actually float on it.

That, of course, led in for the next up-sell:

- Meryl, which of the floats will you be getting today?

After I settled on a float, the skilled sales person asked:

- Do you already have a pump that will work with that?

All this time he was taking my selections to the counter. He then pointed out:

- Meryl, you mentioned that you live in the mountains. That water will get chilly as it cools off at night. You want a cover to keep some of the warmth in, and keep the debris out.

- Do you want me to help you pick out the best water toys for your needs?

I walked out with my arms filled with far more than I had intended to buy, and I was glad that I did. My sales representative was a service professional. He anticipated needs, and made sure I got all those needs met from him, not somewhere else. I offer my compliments to the management of KB Toys in Colorado Springs.

Questions to Focus on the Value of Solving the Problem

You may think that by now both you and they are painfully aware of the problem, and it is time to look for solutions. Take one more step first. Help them to envision life with their problem solved. The next set of PowerPhrases addresses the importance of solving the problem. Help them understand how much better things will be when their problems are solved. Once problems and their implications are determined, use PowerPhrases to Focus on the Value of Solving the Problem, such as:

Help them to envision life with their problem solved.

• How much would you save if you could...?

• Imagine if this problem was solved...

• How useful would it be for you to be able to...?

• If we could ___, how much would that increase your volume?

• If I could show you a way to...

• How important is it that you...?

• How else would it help you to be able to...?

• If I could help you to___, what could you do that you can't do now?

• What high-priority projects could you free yourself up for if you did not have to spend as much time on...?

• What could you do with the savings?

- What would it be worth to you to...?
- How would (increased output) affect (your profitability)?

Help the buyer feel the need to solve their problem. Only then will they care at all about the solutions you offer.

Demonstrating Value

You can easily demonstrate value without creating resistance if you do an excellent job of uncovering needs and selling the buyer on the value of solving the problem. Now you are ready to demonstrate the features and the benefits of what you offer.

Features tell you the facts and characteristics of what you offer. Some features are: the number of pages in a book, the number of minutes included in your phone plan and the amount of memory in a computer. Features are about you and your product.

You can easily demonstrate value without creating resistance if you do an excellent job of uncovering needs and selling the buyer on the value of solving the problem.

True benefits address a need that the buyer has clearly stated they want to resolve. Since they have already told you that they want to solve these problems, expressing true benefits prevents objections. Preventing objections eliminates the need to solve objections.

To express benefits, use a **PowerPhrase to Communicate Benefits**, such as:

- This gives you the ___ you asked for.
- Our widgets meet your specifications.
- This is comfortably within the budget range you have given us.
- We can meet your stated timetable.
- You have said that ___ is important, and we meet your need for ___ by___.

You won't need as many PowerPhrases for describing benefits if you have effectively established the need.

Overcoming Objections

In *Spin Selling*, Neil Rackham asserts that most objections are created when the seller offers solutions too soon. Lay the groundwork first, and brush up on PowerPhrases to handle the objections that you do get.

When they object to price, use a **PowerPhrase to Overcome the Price Objection**, such as:

- What were you planning to pay?

- Why do you say that?

- We can lower the price, but it would require us to eliminate features from the package to do that. Is that acceptable to you?

- What are you comparing it to?

- Does your company always offer the cheapest price? Will you agree that price is not always the only consideration?

- My grandmother used to say that quality is remembered long after cost is forgotten.

- What is the cost of (their problem)?

- Is money the only problem here?

- I hear that from time to time from people before they invest. I never hear that from those who have made the investment.

- Let's bring it down to the cost per day.

- Have you ever paid more than you planned for something you wanted and been glad that you did?

If their objection is that they want to stay with their current supplier, use a **PowerPhrase to Convince Them to Change Suppliers**, such as:

- If I can show you that ours is better, you would want to consider changing or at least sampling what we offer, wouldn't you?

- Is it worth the trouble to change if we offer more?

Objections are created when the seller offers solutions too soon. Lay the groundwork first.

133

- I appreciate your loyalty. I believe you deserve to have a better (service, product).

- Isn't your first loyalty to the company?

- Times have changed, and what worked before may not be what is best now.

- Why not give us a small order to check us out?

- Many of our best customers were reluctant to make the change at first. May I tell you why they are glad that they switched?

- Is there anything about your current supplier that you are not totally happy with? If we could eliminate the problem, wouldn't it be worth considering?

- That's why I need to work extra hard to earn and keep your business.

- Why not give us a chance?

- Change is not comfortable, but it is necessary to stay ahead of the competition.

- Wouldn't it make sense to have an alternative source?

- I am not asking for all of your business here.

Often potential buyers will tell you that they need to think it over because they have not yet heard what they need to be ready to buy.

Another common objection is the "think it over" objection.

Following a strategy similar to the one employed in negotiation processes, use a **PowerPhrase to Overcome the Think It Over Objection,** such as:

- Can you think it over out loud so I can help?

- What do we need to think about?

- What concerns do you have?

- Let's think about it together.

- What do you need from me that would enable you to make a decision now?

- It is possible to think too long. Procrastination can cost money.

- What is your reason for saying that?
- Is there anything I haven't explained well enough?
- You want to think about it? Many people do, and what they consistently find is that their greatest regret is that they did not act sooner.

While the need to reflect on a deal can be legitimate, often potential buyers will tell you that they need to think it over because they have not yet heard what they need to be ready to buy. The above PowerPhrases will help you uncover the real issues.

Closing Phrases

Closing phrases begin with trial closes. These are questions that examine the readiness of the buyer to take action. If you get a yes, you have a sale. If you get a no, you gain information that tells you where you need to focus to reach the sale. Test their readiness in a way that does not force them to take a concrete stand. If you go for a firm commitment too soon, they might feel backed into a corner that they cannot come out of without losing face.

Trial closes examine the readiness of the buyer to take action.

Some **Trial PowerPhrase Closes to Test the Readiness of the Buyer,** are:

- What do you think of what I've told you so far?
- Which version best suits your needs?
- On a scale of 1 to 10, with 10 being ready to invest, where are you? What would it take to get you to a 10?
- Do you prefer this one or that one?
- Wouldn't you agree that this is what you want?
- Do you agree this meets all of the specifications you provided?
- I believe that this meets your needs. Do you agree?
- Why not give it a try?

- Does it make you feel secure to have something that will allow you to...?
- Does this meet all the needs you described?
- What can I do to get your business?
- If you were me, what would you do now?
- Do you need to consult anyone before placing an order?
- This is what you want, isn't it?
- Are there any questions I haven't answered?
- What do you think?

If you get a positive response to these questions, you have a sale. Go for the actual close. At this point, do not hint or beat around the bush.

Clearly ask, using a **PowerPhrase to Close the Sale**, such as:

Before you leave a sales call, use a PowerPhrase to ask for referrals.

- How do you spell your name?
- How do you want to take care of the cost?
- Will that be cash or charge?
- Let's get started.
- Let's make the decision now.
- If you want it, you've got it.
- I just need you to okay this right here.
- I'll keep the paperwork as simple as possible.
- Let's get the paperwork started now.
- Let's wrap it up so we can lock in your rate.

Congratulations! You PowerPhrased your way into a successful sale! You're done now, right?

Well, not quite. You still need to ask for referrals.

PowerPhrases to Request Referrals

Of course, what you REALLY want to do now is to get out of there fast before they change their minds, grab a cool one, sit back and tell your friends about the big one you caught.

It's not time for that just yet. Before you leave, use a **PowerPhrase to Ask for Referrals,** such as:

- Whom do you know who also could benefit from this service?

- I would appreciate the names of some of your acquaintances who could find value in what I offer. Can you provide that?

- Before I leave, I need one more thing from you. Will you please tell me whom else you know...?

- If you were me, whom else would you call?

NOW you can get out of there and celebrate! You earned it!

Celebrate! You earned it!

EXERCISES

I have a warning for you before you begin this exercise. It might seem laborious and tedious. I thought that when I first did it, but it helped me to realize where I was unprepared for the selling that I do. After I set out the exercises for you, I apply the exercises with an example from my own career. If you get lost, use that as a reference.

Step 1. Think about a product or service you offer. List five features of this product.

1. _____

2. _____

3. _____

4. _____

5. _____

Step 2. Next, list five benefits in terms of problems the features can solve for a buyer.

1. _____

2. _____

3. _____

4. _____

5. _____

Step 3. What need would make a buyer care about those benefits?

1. _____

_____

2. _____

_____

3. _____

_____

4. _____

_____

5. _____

_____

Step 4. What situations would lead to those needs?

1. _____

_____

2. _____

_____

3. _____

_____

4. _____

_____

5. _____

_____

Step 5. What PowerPhrases could you use to determine their situations and needs?

1. _____

_____

2. _____

_____

3. _____

_____

4. _____

_____

5. _____

_____

Step 6. What PowerPhrases could you use to uncover the problems?

1. _____

_____

2. _____

_____

3. _____

_____

4. _____

_____

5. _____

_____

Step 7. What PowerPhrases could you use to clarify those problems?

1. _____

_____

2. _____

_____

3. _____

_____

4. _____

_____

5. _____

_____

Step 8. They need to feel the full implications of their problem before they are motivated to solve it. What PowerPhrases would you use to uncover those implications?

1. _____

_____

2. _____

_____

3. _____

_____

4. _____

_____

5. _____

_____

Step 9. The next step is to get them to focus on the importance and value of solving the problem. What PowerPhrases do you use for that?

1. _____

_____

2. _____

_____

3. _____

_____

4. _____

_____

5. _____

_____

Step 10. Now they are ready to hear the benefits. How can you express the benefits in a way that ties into their specific needs?

1. _____

_____

2. _____

_____

3. _____

_____

4. _____

_____

5. _____

_____

Sample Exercise

At seminars, I sell a powerful tape set called *12 Secrets to High Self-Esteem* by Linda Larsen.[5] I honestly believe that if people do not walk out of the room with those tapes, it is because I did not use my PowerPhrases well enough. Here is how I apply the process.

Step 1. Features:
1. Six cassettes.
2. Workbook.
3. 12 specific steps.
4. Uses stories, research and examples.
5. Describes goal setting.

Step 2. Benefits, problems it can solve:
1. Fear of asking for what you want.
2. Putting yourself down.
3. Overreacting emotionally.
4. Confusion about what you want in life.
5. Settling for less than you deserve.

Step 3. In order to care, a buyer would have to feel a need for:
1. Assertive communications skills.
2. Self-acceptance.
3. Emotional control.
4. Goal clarification.
5. A sense of deserving.

Step 4. Situations that would lead to these needs are:
1. No good training or role models. Being told "Don't you talk back to me!"
2. Critical people.
3. Emotionally repressive or reactive environments. Environments where telling the truth about your feelings is unsafe.
4. Others expecting their needs to be consistently first.
5. Experiencing conditional love. Abusive relationships.

---

[5] *12 Secrets of High Self-Esteem*, Larsen, Linda, SkillPath Publications

Step 5. PowerPhrases to Determine Situation:

• How did you learn to ask for what you want?

• Were any of your immediate family critical of you?

• Are you able to express emotions calmly in an honest and open way?

• Have you ever been expected to sacrifice what you want for someone else and later resented it?

• Have you ever felt taken advantage of?

Step 6. PowerPhrases to Uncover the Problem:

• Does lack of assertive communication skills ever cause a problem for you?

• Do you tell yourself the same things those critical people tell or told you?

• What challenges has lack of emotional control created for you?

• How satisfied are you with your history of setting personal goals and reaching them?

• What has being taken advantage of cost you?

Step 7. PowerPhrases to Clarify Problems:

• What other problems have you had due to lack of assertiveness?

• What has been the result of those negative conversations in your head?

• Is emotional control a problem for you in other areas of your life as well?

• What about your lack of goal setting worries you?

• Have you had other difficulties with being taken advantage of?

Step 8. PowerPhrases to Reveal Implications of Problems:

• Has your lack of assertiveness created problems for your family as well?

• Do the negative conversations in your head keep you from going after what you want?

• Does that emotional control problem ever cause your staff to be afraid to discuss issues with you?

• Does your lack of direction frustrate your family?

• Does being vulnerable to being taken advantage of ever cause you to keep people at arms length?

Step 9. PowerPhrases to Focus on the Value of Solving the Problem:

• How important is it that you learn to assert yourself?

• What difference would it make in your life if you were not second-guessing yourself?

• If you had better emotional control, how would your life be better?

• If you began setting goals toward the things you dream about, where do you picture yourself in five years?

• How would your life improve if you learned to set clear boundaries?

Step 10. PowerPhrases to Sell the Benefits of Your Product:

• Secret number nine in the *12 Secrets to High Self-Esteem* is "Communicating with Confidence." It gives you the exact assertiveness skills you said you need to...

• You can get (what they said they would get if they stopped second-guessing themselves) by investing in the *12 Secrets to High Self-Esteem.* "Accessing Your Internal Wisdom" is secret number two. That and secret number four, "Accepting Yourself and Letting Go of the Past" will give you the self acceptance you said would free you to do what you want.

• Linda Larsen will tell you exactly what to do to get the emotional control you said would help you (the benefits they mentioned) with secret 5, "Managing Your Emotions."

• You said you see yourself being ___ in five years if you improve your goal setting. Linda Larsen will tell you exactly how to get there.

• The *12 Secrets* will show you how to get that life you envision when you learn to set clear boundaries.

Whew! If you are reading this, my guess is you actually walked through the steps with me. Great job! Now your challenge is to walk through those steps with something you want to sell or convince someone of. Using these steps is tedious at first, but over time the framework becomes automatic...and effective!

QUIZ

1. Which type of PowerPhrase needs to be used sparingly and only in the beginning?

2. Which type of PowerPhrase do you need to avoid using too soon in the selling process?

Answers:

1. Situation questions need to be used sparingly and only in the beginning. Too many of these imply that you haven't done your homework.

2. PowerPhrases to communicate benefits need to be reserved until the need is clearly established. Let the buyer "feel their pain" first.

Good Old Boy's Club got you down?
Read, *The Good Old Boys Club: Chipping Away at the Legend
and the Reality* http://www.speakstrong.com/articles/speak-strong/
good-old-boys-tales.html

CHAPTER 7

Small Talk PowerPhrases® to Break the Ice

Do you look forward to social situations where you are expected to strike up conversations with people you do not know? Or would you rather have a tax audit, drink cod liver oil, or get a root canal?

If you dread small talk, you are not alone. You may have heard that the greatest fear of most people is speaking in public. Did you know that our second greatest fear is starting a conversation with someone we do not know? If you are not comfortable with small talk, it might help to know that six out of those eight people you meet are not comfortable with it either.

The really good news is that the art of mingling is a learned one. Like any other skill, you can master it. You can learn the lines that melt the ice. I'm talking PowerPhrases here, if you haven't guessed!

Do you think small talk is a waste of time? The truth is that small talk is anything BUT a waste of time. If you have two people with equal skills, who is likely to get the promotion—the one who is shy and retreated, keeping to herself but doing a great job—or the other who jokes easily with the CEO as well as the janitor, knows who to call to get things done in a hurry, and who is on a first name basis with the entire Chamber of Commerce and Rotary club and is also doing a great job? Small talk makes big things happen! Small talk turns strangers into

The second greatest fear of all is starting a conversation with someone we do not know.

acquaintances, and acquaintances into friends. People like doing business with their friends.

How to Begin

The most important PowerPhrase available is the other person's name. Use it freely–and with care. If you meet Susan, David, Barbara and Robert, don't say:

— *Hey Susie!*

— *Nice to meet you Dave!*

— *Barb, how are you?*

— *Bob, it's a pleasure!*

Call them Susan, David, Barbara and Robert until you have been given permission to alter it. If there is any doubt about whether to use first names or surnames, use their surnames–or ask!

Small talk makes big things happen!

Take the time to learn the correct pronunciation. Help them with yours!

Use a **PowerPhrase to Help Others to Pronounce and Remember Your Name,** such as:

• **Hi! I'm Meryl Runion. Meryl rhymes with barrel and Runion rhymes with onion. So if you forget my name, think about a barrel of onions.**

• **I'm Houston Rose. Houston is like the city; Rose is like the flower.**

If you meet someone who has a difficult name, do not pretend that they do not have a name! Take the time to get their name right. If you are unsure of the pronunciation, ask for their help in remembering it.

Simply use a **PowerPhrase to Get Help Remembering a Name,** such as:

• **What a lovely name. I want to be certain that I say it correctly. What tips do you have for me?**

Take the responsibility of names onto yourself. If you

have forgotten someone's name, use a **PowerPhrase to Ask That a Name Be Repeated,** such as:

• I apologize; I've forgotten your name.

• What was your name again?

• You don't happen to remember YOUR name, do you?

• Please help me out. I've gone blank here.

If you think they may have forgotten your name, tell them before they have to ask. Say:

• Janet, Meryl Runion, how are you?

You can also prompt them to tell you their name by greeting them with a reminder of your name.

Learning Names Through Repetition

Repeat their names as much as possible. Don't say:

— *What was that like?*

when you can say:

• Janet, what was that like?

Every time you use their name, it adds to the rapport between you, and it reinforces their name in your mind.

Every time you use their name, it adds to the rapport between you.

Giving More Information in Order to Invite More Information from Them

Be aware that people usually respond in kind to the way we speak to them. If I say:

— *Hi! I'm Meryl!*

they are likely to say:

— *Hi! I'm ___.*

If I say:

• Hi! I'm Meryl Runion and I'm a speaker and an author. I'm here for the first time.

they are likely to say:

- I'm ___ ___, and I work for Widget Wonderland. I've been coming since August.

Now I have some information to work with! I know they work for Widget Wonderland and they have been coming since last August. I can use that to ask questions that will open the conversation up further.

- Widget Wonderland! I haven't been there since it was Widget Wonder World. How has it changed?

- What have you gained from coming here?

Keep going until you forget that small talk is something you're not good at.

The art of mingling is a learned one.

> ### Power Pointer— Small Talk PowerPhrases on an Airplane
>
> *On a flight I took recently, a flight attendant showed a remarkable ability to start conversations. She asked me if my top was silk, and went on to tell me about how her boyfriend put her silk clothes through the washer and dryer. Of course, I had ruined-clothes-stories of my own. She was chatting casually with everyone in the same way.*
>
> *Most of us make similar associations in response to other people, but only a few of us actually think to relay our associations to strangers. This flight attendant's gift was the casualness with which she relayed her inner experience. Her absolute comfort with it made it comfortable for everyone else as well.*

Small talk is much easier if you are interested in what the other person has to say. There is something interesting in everyone. Relax and consider yourself an undercover agent with a mission to find out what is interesting about them.

Starting Conversations With Statements

Do you ever attempt to start a conversation with a statement?

— *Great weather we're having.*

— *The turnout is huge here today!*

If you think you are throwing out a conversational ball that they should pick up and toss back, think again. Statements like these lead nowhere unless you are talking to a small talk genius that knows how to pick the ball up and toss it back. Remember: most people respond at the same level we put things out. Most people will not pick up that ball and toss it back. Give them something they can get their hands on.

The Three-Step Icebreaking Process

Instead of throwing out a statement and hoping that they will pick up on it, use the three-step icebreaking process.

Use the three-step icebreaking process.

1. Make an opening statement.
2. Reveal something (not too personal) about yourself. (Usually they will respond by giving you information about themselves.)
3. Encourage them to reveal something about themselves.

Good opening statements come from observing the environment or the other person. Good disclosure statements come from observing yourself and your thoughts. Good invitation questions come from a genuine interest in the other person and/or the information they can give you.

Put them together into the three-step icebreaking process.

Statement	Disclosure	Invitation
That's a beautiful painting!	I don't know much about art.	What kind of art do you like?
This food is delicious.	I like Indian food.	How about you?
Great house!	I like southwestern styling.	How did you come up with the theme?
The elevator is taking forever.	I'm going to be late to my seminar.	What are you here for?
Great weather we're having.	This weather makes me wish I still had my motorcycle.	How do you take advantage of weather like this?
The turnout is huge here today!	I came to hear the talk on eWidgets.	What brings you here?

Open-Ended Questions

Closed-ended questions give the other person nowhere to go.

Have you ever attempted to initiate small talk with closed-ended questions that give the other person nowhere to go? Don't ask:

— *What do you do?*

— *How was your vacation?*

— *Where do you live?*

— *How are you?*

These questions solicit one-word responses. They are useful if you are looking for specific information, but they do not draw the other person out. They are only useful as small talk if you follow them up with open-ended questions. Otherwise, after they've said I'm an attorney, fine, downtown and great, what are you left with?

Open-ended questions are more effective. These are the questions that require a more extensive response. Open-ended questions are **PowerPhrases That Get a Conversation Going,** such as:

- What led you to do the kind of work you are doing?
- What did you like best about your vacation?
- What do you like about where you live?
- Get me up-to-date on what's been happening for you lately.
- How did you get started in your business?
- What do you enjoy most about the work you do?
- What advice would you give someone just starting in your business?
- How has your industry changed lately?
- What separates you from your competition?

Before you speak, ask yourself how *you* would respond to the remark if someone made it to you. If the answer is that your response would not provide much new information, find another way to express yourself.

Closed-ended questions often begin with:

— *How long...*

— *Have you...*

— *Do you...*

— *Would you...*

— *Did you...*

Open-ended questions require more extensive responses.

Open-ended questions often begin with **PowerPhrase Sentence Stems to Open a Conversation,** such as:

- What about...?
- Explain...
- Tell me about...
- What do you...?
- What got you...?
- Describe...

Beware of questions that begin with why. "Why" questions can trigger a defensive response in your listener.

Develop a 10-Second Commercial for Yourself

Prepare yourself for meeting strangers by planning a 10-second commercial for yourself. When you introduce yourself, give additional information. That gives them something to work with in developing and keeping a conversation going. Chances are great that they will then offer more information back.

If David says he is a systems engineer, his listener might not know what to say next. Listeners might have an easier time if he uses a **10-Second Commercial PowerPhrase,** such as:

Plan a 10-second commercial for yourself.

- **I'm a systems engineer. When someone wants to do something the computer refuses to do, they call me. My job is to analyze how to get the computer to do it.**

When I explain that I am a speaker and an author, people often do not have much of a picture of what I do. They have more to work with if I use my **10-Second Commercial PowerPhrase.**

- **I motivate people to speak directly and clearly through my books, newsletters and seminars.**

You know from experience what common questions people ask you, so answer those questions for them up front. Prepare in advance.

You may have met network-marketing people who respond to the question, "What do you do?" by saying:

— *I help people start businesses.*

This is misleading and unclear. You want to add clarity, not confusion.

A good **10-Second Commercial PowerPhrase** for this situation might be:

• I have a wellness business. I market magnets for health and pain control, and I help others with their wellness businesses as well.

The main key is to prepare. When you go to an event where there is likely to be small talk, plan your PowerPhrases in advance. Read the paper, survey the environment, and come up with interesting topics for discussion.

Know What You Have to Give and What You Want to Get

Go into networking situations and make small talk with a clear idea of what you want to accomplish–and what you have to give. Every person you meet needs to know something that you already know, and every person you meet knows something that you need to know. If you begin your small talk with a clear idea of how you want the conversation to end up, you are likely to have satisfying results. Be straightforward about what you are looking for by using a **PowerPhrase to Make Your Agenda Known,** such as:

Begin your small talk with a clear idea of how you want the conversation to end up.

• I want to get to know you better because...

• I am here because I am looking for information about...

• I am looking for information about... Do you know someone who can help me?

You are creating a give and get situation. If no one makes his or her needs known, no one will give and no one will get.

There is nothing small and insignificant about small talk. Take the time to learn the art. And before you attend a networking situation, be certain to prepare.

Exercises

1. Turn the following closed-ended questions into open-ended questions.
Are things changing a lot in your department?

_____

_____

Is your job challenging?

_____

_____

Do you come here often?

_____

_____

2. Create a 10-Second Commercial for Yourself

_____

_____

_____

_____

_____

_____

_____

_____

_____

_____

_____

_____

_____

Chapter 8

PowerPhrases® at Work: Managing Your Boss

Have you seen the lists of buzzwords that you can choose from if you want to sound "erudite"? There are three columns of words. You are instructed to pick a word from each column, and you end up with statements like:

— *ineluctable semidiurnal factionalism, or:*

— *facilitating cognizant circumlocution.*

The results are big expressions with very little meaning.

Fortunately the trend in governments and businesses is toward simpler and more straightforward communications. There are plenty of exceptions however. Until recently the Minneapolis airport played a message that said:

— *Attention passengers! Please carefully control your bags to avoid the unauthorized introduction of foreign objects by unknown persons.*

I always picture a harried passenger shouting "Down bags!" to their out-of-control bags. There is an "unknown person," dressed in black and wearing a ski mask, introducing foreign objects–Chinese coins and Russian nesting dolls–into the out-of-control bags. How about a simple "Watch your bags so that strangers don't put anything in them"?

That sounds like a PowerPhrase to me!

The trend in governments and businesses is toward simpler and more straightforward communications.

Your business communications need to be clear and direct at work, starting at the interview.

PowerPhrases at the Interview

Does it seem odd to you that PowerPhrases have a place in a job interview? Job interviews are about selling yourself. How can you sell yourself with memorized phrases that you read in a book? The answer is that you don't simply memorize anything. You adapt the PowerPhrases to your own situation. The PowerPhrases get you started-and you take it from there. You will do much better if you are prepared for common interview questions.

Power Preparation for the Interview

In addition to preparing your PowerPhrases, learn everything you can about the company. Read their web pages, annual report, journals and newsletters. Talk to everyone that you know who knows anything about the company. Also be certain to request a job description for the position you are applying for so you can prepare to show them how you can meet their needs.

Prepare responses in advance for common interview questions.

PowerPhrase Responses to Common Interview Questions

A very popular ice-breaking interview question is: "Tell me about yourself."

Get creative! You don't need to respond mechanically by saying something like:

— *My name is... and I come from...*

— *My hobbies are...*

— *What I like to do best is...*

Instead, be specific and use a **PowerPhrase for Describing Yourself,** such as:

- **My strengths are... An example is...**

- **My accomplishments are... For example...**

- **My greatest area of knowledge is... I have used this by...**

Or ask:

- **Is there a particular area you would like for me to discuss?**

Use strong words, and then illustrate them with specifics.

When asked why you are in the job market, don't say:

— *They didn't appreciate me where I was.*

— *My boss was an idiot.*

— *I did not like it.*

— *I was personally responsible for the company declaring bankruptcy.*

Use strong words, and then illustrate them with specifics.

Instead use a **PowerPhrase for Explaining Why You Are in the Job Market,** such as:

- **I have a plan for my career. I need a place that offers opportunity for growth.**

- **I am ready for a new set of challenges.**

- **I want a job that I can give my all to and that I can stay in for a long time. I'm looking for the right opportunity.**

When they ask why you are the best person for the job, don't say:

— *I think this is a good place to work.*

— *Nothing else looked interesting.*

— *I'm out of work.*

— *I don't know for sure that I am because I haven't met the other candidates.*

159

Instead, use a **PowerPhrase for Explaining Why You Are the Best for the Job,** such as:

- I put my heart into everything I do. For example…

- I thrive on problem solving and challenges. For example…

- You need someone who can produce results. My track record shows that I am that kind of a person.

- This job is exactly what I want. What I can do for you is…

- My experience demonstrates my versatility.

Even if you are uncertain about being the best candidate, speak with confidence.

Even if you are uncertain, speak with confidence.

Power Thinking to the Rescue— Replace Limiting Thinking With Power Thoughts

You want to have an attitude of confidence at the interview, and the attitude you project will be a reflection of your thoughts.

Don't think:

— *Why would they choose me?*

— *I need to prove myself to them.*

— *They aren't going to like me.*

These thoughts will make you appear weak and needy. Instead, think:

- I have much to offer.

- This is an opportunity to find out if we are a match.

- I am here to learn about them as well as for them to learn about me.

The second set of thoughts will make you appear confident and calm.

Asking the Interviewer PowerPhrase Questions

Do you dread job interviews? Think of them as two-way streets rather than one-way interrogations. Job interviews are not just about the potential employer finding out if you meet their needs. Both the employer and the job seeker want a good match. You're not just along for the ride at an interview. Be prepared to shine. Also, be prepared to seek the information you need to make a knowledgeable career decision. When the interviewer asks if you have questions, don't say:

— No. (*Implies that you don't really care.*)

— Not really. (*Now you sound like you don't care and you are uncertain as well!*)

Avoid asking questions that imply that you are only interested in what you can get. Also avoid questions that have a negative spin and questions that indicate that you haven't done your homework, such as:

— *How much will you pay me? (Only interested in what you can get)*

— *What happened to the person who had the job before me? (Negative)*

— *What does this company do, anyway? (Under-prepared)*

Be prepared with **PowerPhrase Questions for the Interviewer**, such as:

• What else can I tell you about my qualifications?

• What are the initial responsibilities of the position?

• What problems face your staff?

• What is the growth potential in this position?

• How long have you been here? What do *you* like about the company?

• What would the characteristics and experience of the perfect applicant be?

Be prepared to seek the information you need to make a knowledgeable career decision.

• What is the mission of the company?

Show your interest and initiative in the questions that you ask. If you do not ask questions, you imply that you take whatever someone hands you. Your first job is to be responsive to the interviewer. Your second job is to guide the interview as needed.

When the interview is winding down, use PowerPhrases to get closure.

Going for Closure With PowerPhrases Without Being Pushy

Do not leave the interview without going for some closure. Toward the end of the interview, create a sense of value and urgency by using **PowerPhrases That Push for Action.**

• Are there any qualities you are looking for that you haven't seen in me?

• Is there anything you want to know that I haven't told you?

• What can I tell you that would prompt you to make an offer now?

• Can you offer me the job?

If they say no, ask:

• Can you refer me to someone who can use my skills?

If they say they will consider the application and get back to you, say:

• When can I expect your decision?

• If I have not heard from you by then, may I call you?

Show your interest and initiative in the questions that you ask. If you do not ask questions, you imply that you take whatever someone hands you.

A PowerPhrase to the Rescue! Take Charge Without Taking Control!

I was interviewing for a job that I was seriously under-qualified for. The interviewer was talking about everything but the job! I felt discouraged and out-of-control. I did not get the job. I was told what I could do to improve my qualifications and that if I cared to reapply in about a year, they would reconsider my application.

One year later and slightly more qualified, I interviewed again with the same interviewer. It was like history revisited. The interviewer was off on a tangent. This time, rather than panic, I took charge. This time I said:

- **I want to focus on the job, because this is what I want to do.**

I could see it in the interviewer's eyes. That was the moment I got the job.

Many employers are looking for assertive candidates. That can be demonstrated by how assertive you are willing to be with them.

Most employers are looking for assertive candidates. This can be demonstrated by how assertive you are willing to be with them.

PowerPhrases for When You Are New on the Job

Once you have the job, use PowerPhrases to help you to integrate into your new environment. While you want to look good those early weeks, you don't want to alienate anyone or come across as arrogant.

Don't say:

— *That's not how we did it at Widget Direct.*

Use **PowerPhrases for Your Early Days on the Job**, such as:

- I'm looking forward to understanding how you do it here.
- I am happy to do it your way.

Don't say:

— *Let me tell you all about myself!*

Say:

- I'm anxious to learn about you.

Don't say:

— *I can figure it out myself.*

Say:

- I need your help.
- I need your advice.
- I can use some input here.

PowerPhrases help you to integrate into your new environment.

When you make inevitable errors or don't know what is expected of you, avoid saying:

— *I'm only human!*

— *Be nice to me, I'm new.*

— *I haven't got the experience.*

Use **PowerPhrases for Reminding Them That You Are New,** such as:

- I apologize. I am still in my learning curve.
- I just made another mistake to learn from.
- That is the last time I will make that mistake!

Power Pointer—Admit Fault When Appropriate

Lisa was contracted by a bank to be a mystery shopper to discover what services competing banks offer. Unfortunately, her report got forwarded to one of the bank representatives that she had been investigating. The representative sent a reply email asking what was going on and if Lisa was legitimately interested in her services. Lisa was embarrassed, and wondered how to respond.

I shared the following three-step process that research shows mends fences as quickly as possible. Say:

- **I'm sorry.**
- **Please forgive me.**
- **It will never happen again.**

If you really messed up, follow this with:

- **How can I make it up to you?**

Lisa made her call immediately. The representative completely understood and Lisa was very glad that she did not attempt to cover over the truth. Don't hide — admit the truth!

Do not wait for your coworkers to tell you everything. **Use PowerPhrase Questions for New Employees,** such as:

- How can I help?
- What more can I do?
- How am I doing?
- What are my priorities?

Time spent getting to know your boss is time well invested.

PowerPhrases for Your Supervisor

In the Beginning

Your first meeting with your boss sets the tone for your entire working relationship, so plan ahead for that. Much of the initial weeks is about getting to know your boss. Time spent getting to know your boss is time well invested. Since you are likely to get a new boss every six months, it is important to know the PowerPhrases involved. Do not expect to be at full capacity your first day. Do not say:

— *This isn't what I was hired to do.*

— *When are you going to tell me what to do?*

— *I don't have a plan, that's your job.*

Use PowerPhrases for Meeting Your Boss, such as:

• I'm _____ and am looking forward to working with you.

• Can you give me a quick sense of the priorities in the department?

• When you have a chance, I have some action ideas of my own that I would like your opinion on.

Every manager has their own idea of how things should be done. You need to study your manager's style. Ask questions about how your boss wants things.

First you learn them – then they learn you.

Don't say:

— *This isn't how my old boss did things.*

— *You need to tell me what to do.*

— *I have my own way of doing things.*

Instead, ask questions and make remarks such as the following **PowerPhrases for Getting to Know Your Boss.**

• What more can I do to help you?

• I look forward to understanding your style.

• I want to learn what you need from me.

• May I take notes?

• What did you particularly like about the way the last person who had this position did the job?

• I'd like to know more about you in order to best understand how to work with you.

> ### Power Pointer— First You Learn Them — Then They Learn You.
>
> *One group of assistants agreed: when you begin a job, you need to learn your boss' style. Then help the boss learn yours. Once you know your boss' preferences, strengths and limitations, develop systems to work with them. Once they are developed, you can introduce them to your supervisor bit by bit.*

Making Suggestions to Your Boss

Some bosses are very open to new ideas. Others like to think that everything is their idea. There are ways to make recommendations that leave them thinking that they thought of it.

If they like to think that they thought of everything, don't say:

— *My advice is…*

— *Obviously you should…*

— *Try this…*

Some bosses like to think that everything is their idea.

Instead, use a **PowerPhrase for Making Suggestions to the Boss**, such as:

• **Have you considered…?**

• **Something you said the other day got me thinking…**

• **I'd like your opinion about what I did with the concepts you and I discussed last month.**

167

> ### Power Pointer— Always Look for Something to Agree About.
>
> *Bob had a product line designed exclusively for his department. When Bob's director encouraged selling the line through the call center, Bob said:*
>
> • Short-term that makes a lot of sense. Here are the problems I see long-term.
>
> *Note Bob refrained from saying:*
>
> *– That's short-term smart and long-term dumb.*
>
> *His opening acknowledged the validity of the perspective but led into the second part, which outlined what the boss had not considered.*

The better you word your disagreement, the easier it is to keep the disagreement from becoming a conflict.

Do you hesitate to offer suggestions when you completely disagree with the boss? According to my informal polls, about one out of three adults equate disagreement with conflict. The better worded a disagreement is, the easier it is to bypass the sense of being in conflict.

Don't say:

— *You're wrong.*

— *You shouldn't see it that way.*

— *I disagree.*

Instead use a **PowerPhrase for Disagreeing With the Boss,** such as:

• Help me to understand how you reached that conclusion.

• I wonder if we have the same information. My information leads me to a different conclusion.

• I want to give my best here. I can support you better if we can resolve these differences first.

Replace Limiting Thinking With Power Thoughts

If you view your disagreement as a conflict, conflict is more likely to result. Watch out for the thoughts:

— *It's me against him/her.*

— *I'm not a team player if I refuse.*

Think:

• We can work toward an effective solution here.

• My assessment of what is possible is important information for the boss.

• My needs are important too.

Have a fallback position if the boss does not appreciate your candor.

• I know that you are the boss and I will do whatever you say.

Please note that if you find yourself using your fallback phrase a lot, you may not be in the correct position for you.

It is not your manager's job to keep track of what assignments you have been given.

Refusing Assignments

You are hired to do what management asks of you, so it is reasonable to wonder…do you have the right to refuse an assignment? Absolutely! Not only do you have the right, you have the obligation to prioritize responsibilities so the important work gets the attention it requires. It is not your manager's job to keep track of what assignments you have been given. Often they don't know what else you have to do. When you refuse an assignment, don't say:

— *I can't.*

— *I don't have the skills.*

— *I'm overloaded already.*

— *Why do I get all the crummy assignments?*

— *What do I look like here, Wonder Woman/ Superman?*

Begin by clarifying the request. Ask detailed questions so you know the scope.

Be certain to ask the following **PowerPhrases for Clarifying an Assignment**, such as:

• **I need more information. What is the deadline?**

• **I need more information. What budget is allotted?**

• **I need more information. What are the specifications?**

• **Which is the most binding of the three, and how flexible are the others?**

Sometimes you need to say 'no' to an assignment. PowerPhrases show you how.

If you decide from the answers that you cannot carry out the assignment, use a **PowerPhrase for Refusing an Assignment**. This phrase will follow the same format for saying no as was described in Chapter 3. Begin with an acknowledgment, explain the situation, and reaffirm the relationship by presenting options.

Power Pointer— How to Say NO to an Assignment.

A subscriber sent me the following brilliant example of how to say no to an assignment.

Recently my supervisor volunteered us for another time-consuming project. He came to my office and said: "You will make this work easily and efficiently just as you have with your other duties." I asked him:

• **What projects of mine do you see as being a priority?**

He listed off the most important tasks. I then asked:

- **Which duty could I delegate in order to have adequate time to make my project successful?**

He stared at me dumbfounded for almost an entire minute (47 seconds as I watched the clock above his head) before he answered: "None." I told him that I could not give the project the time and attention it needed to be a success with my current duties. I then asked how we might be able to split the duties between some of our personnel. We talked for another fifteen minutes before we had a plan written out. We now have implemented the new changes and things are running fairly smoothly. I am proud that I was able to tell my supervisor NO without using the "N" word.

Had she accepted the project without question, it would have been a disaster not only for her, but for her boss as well. She spoke well, wisely, and to the benefit of all involved.

Use the three-step process for saying "No" when you need to refuse an assignment.

The Three-Step Process for Saying No to Refuse Assignments

Acknowledge	Circumstance	Transform
This project is so important it needs someone who can make it his or her top priority.	I have the following projects and dead-lines…	Let me look into it and come back with a list of questions and recommendations.
I am flattered that you considered me for this assignment.	After reviewing it I see some problems that need to be reviewed before proceeding.	Let's discuss the problems I see and what options we can create.
I take this project very seriously.	The risks I see in my taking this on are…	If we can resolve these I will be happy to take this on.
I prefer to say yes to every assignment you offer me.	My concerns are…	What can I put aside to free myself up for this?

You can also use a one or two-part format to refuse the assignment.

Saying No in One or Two Parts

Acknowledge	Circumstance	Transform
		Let me look into it and come back with a list of questions and recommendations.
This project is so important it needs someone who can make it his or her top priority.		Have you considered asking…?
	I have reviewed the assignment and see that we have some problems that need to be resolved before proceeding.	What can I put aside to clear my schedule enough to take this on?
		What can I put aside to free myself up for this?
	My policy is not to take on a project without making the risks known. Some of the risks I see to you here are...	

Before you commit to an assignment you cannot carry out, use PowerPhrases to ask questions.

Remember. A PowerPhrase is as strong as it needs to be and no stronger. Be clear with your manager while you avoid sounding like you believe you are in charge.

Handling Multiple Supervisors

Do you work for more than one supervisor? Is it a nightmare of competing requests? If so, develop a system that your supervisors agree to in advance. Refer to that system to keep you out of the middle.

As tempting as it is, refrain from saying:

— *Take a number.*

— *I can't help you.*

— *Your project is not my only priority.*

— *You're not the only one I support here.*

Instead, use a **PowerPhrase for Managing Work From Multiple Bosses**, such as:

Acknowledge	Circumstance	Transform
I would love to help.	Mary has already scheduled my time.	Why not talk to Mary? Perhaps she can give you priority.
	According to the system we established, I prioritize work by...	I will be able to get to this by....

Replace Limiting Thinking With Power Thoughts

When managers conflict on priorities, stay out of the middle.

You may think:

— *I've got to balance all their conflicting demands.*

— *It's up to me to figure this out.*

You are better off thinking:

• Their conflicts are between them and I will allow them to resolve them.

• We can develop systems that everyone agrees to and I will follow them.

Develop a system to prioritize work that both you and your boss can agree to.

Meeting With Your Managers

Is getting a meeting with your boss harder than getting a recount in Florida? Meeting with staff is a high-payoff activity for bosses, but your supervisor may need to be convinced. Ask for the meetings you need with your boss, but do it with grace. Refrain from complaining:

— *You never have enough time for me.*

— *Everything else comes first.*

— *It seems like I don't matter.*

Instead, use a **PowerPhrase for Requesting Regular Meetings With Your Boss,** such as:

• If we meet for ten minutes on a daily basis, I won't need to interrupt you as frequently throughout the day.

Ask for the meetings you need with your boss, but do it with grace.

• I have found in the past that meeting on a daily basis increases my productivity and allows me to stay in tune with you. It helps me make you look good.

• Let's try meeting on a daily basis, monitor the results and see if it is something we would like to continue.

Also, advocate for regular performance reviews. You need regular reviews to make your supervisors aware of the ways you contribute to the company. In addition, it is in your interest to find out where you fall short of the supervisor's expectations early enough to use the information for change. Don't say:

— *I'm afraid I may be doing something wrong.*

— *You promised!*

— *I'm low on the totem poll here.*

Instead use a **PowerPhrase for Requesting a Performance Review,** such as:

• To give my best possible I want to set a time to

review my progress and set some goals. When can we do that?

• I work best with regular feedback, and I want to do the best job possible here.

Replace Limiting Thinking With Power Thoughts

Performance reviews are opportunities to advance. Don't think:

— *I'm afraid of what they might say.*

Think:

• **This is a chance to get credit for what I've done and learn what I need to improve.**

The International Association of Administrative Professionals recommends that you gather your information for your supervisor, and have a cover letter saying something like:

• Thank you for your role in helping me perform so well in this past year. Some things I appreciate about our working relationship are:...[6]

Be an active participant at your performance review! Performance reviews are wonderful ways to get what you need. Use them to get your accomplishments noticed. Accept praise, consider the criticism and be prepared with facts that make note of your accomplishments.

Use **PowerPhrases for Making Your Accomplishments Known in a Performance Review**, such as:

• May I begin by telling you the accomplishments I am most proud of?

• Here is how I made money for the company...

• Here is how I saved money for the company...

You need regular performance reviews to make your supervisors aware of your contributions to the company.

---

[6] International Association of Administrative Professionals (IAAP) website

- Here are three problems I faced last year. What I did to resolve them is...

- I want to invite you to tell me what you are most pleased about.

Be sure to use the review as an opportunity to find out what the boss sees as good performance, and what it takes to get a promotion.

- My understanding is that my priority is to (reconfigure widgets). I have been assembling 257 per day. Is this the best use of my time?

- I want to know in detail what the measurements of good performance are.

- What can I do differently to meet your requirements?

Even weaknesses can be turned in to strengths at performance reviews.

Be an active participant at your performance review!

- Here are some of the areas I have been weak. Here is what I am doing to overcome them.

- I realized I was weak in accounting so I took classes.

Summarize your understanding.

- My understanding is that I am in good shape and you want me to...(start assembling wind-up widgets). Is this correct?

These phrases help you look good-and they help you be good by understanding expectations.

Accepting Feedback

You can expect that during your performance review, you will receive some praise and you can expect that you will receive some criticism. How do you accept praise and criticism from your employer? When praised, don't deflect the compliment by saying:

— *It was nothing.*

— *It was my team. (Unless it was!)*

— *You're right; I did do a great job! Let me tell you about the 333,488 obstacles that I overcame single-handedly. Number one, I…*

Instead, use a **PowerPhrase for Accepting Compliments From the Boss,** such as:

• Thank you. That means a lot, especially from you.

• Thank you. It helped that I had such great support from my team.

• Thank you. I feel great about it too.

• Thank you for noticing.

How do you respond to criticism from a supervisor? Be very careful to avoid arguing. Avoid words like:

— *You're wrong.*

— *You don't have a clue what I do for you.*

— *After all that I do for you, all you notice are the mistakes.*

— *Whatever you say…*

— *Yeah, but YOU…*

Even weaknesses can be turned in to strengths at performance reviews.

Instead, respond with a **PowerPhrase for Accepting Criticism,** such as:

• I wasn't aware that there was a problem. I want to hear your feedback to understand what needs to be changed.

• I understand why you viewed it that way. Next time, I will handle it by doing… I want to do whatever I can to strengthen our working relationship. I consider us a team.[7]

• I plan to take this information and devise a plan to improve my performance.

One powerful way to respond to criticism is to seek clarification of the speaker's point of view.

• What else would you like to see me do differently?

[7] *How to Prepare for Your Annual Performance Review* By Susan Fenner, Education & Professional Development Manager, IAAP World Headquarters

- What do you mean by...?
- Do I understand you correctly that...?
- What needs to be done at this point?

A performance review is a good time to request the resources you need to do a better job. That doesn't mean you should complain and say:

— *I can't meet my objectives because you...*

— *I am not getting the results I want because I do not have...*

Instead use a **PowerPhrase to Request Resources,** such as:

- A few things that would increase my productivity are...
- My research has shown that these are the costs... and these are the savings... of obtaining the following resources...

Ask for the resources you need in terms of how they will help you to be more effective.

Breaking Bad News to the Boss

Do you ever have bad news to give the boss? It is essential to take accountability and talk about remedies. Avoid saying:

— *That idiot Jenkins withdrew his account. He just wasn't patient enough to see this thing through.*

— *I won't meet the deadline.*

— *I should have...*

Instead, do your homework before speaking. Make sure there really is a problem. Then take immediate action. Come armed with all possible solutions. Look ahead to the future.

Use a **PowerPhrase for Breaking Bad News to the Boss,** such as:

A performance review is a good time to request the resources you need to do a better job.

- **I made a mistake. I did not realize…**(that Jenkins needed more consistent updates than most of our clients require, and I updated him as I do our other clients.) **He…**(became nervous and withdrew his account before our approach had a chance to pay off.) **Some measures I have taken are…**

- **I have some bad news. There have been…**(major delays) **and…**(we are unable to meet the quality requirements within the given deadline.) **Here are three recommendations of how we can address the client's concerns. Number 1….**

- **To do the best job possible, I need one more week.**

- **Next time I will …**

If you want to introduce the subject in a humorously humble way, say:

- **I just made a career-limiting move.**

Admit mistakes and move on to giving your best.

When you break bad news to your boss, come armed with all possible solutions.

Power Tip: Put Things in Context

In "How to Deal With Difficult People," Paul Freid-man tells of an ad executive that mishandled an account. He began his report to the board of directors by placing a black dot on a white sheet. When asked what they saw, they said "a black dot." He replied:

- **Yes, and there is also a large white sheet of paper. Notice when something is blemished we attend to that blemish and overlook the broad background on which it is placed. I hope you keep that background in mind when I make my report this morning.**

This approach shows you how to balance taking responsibility and helping them maintain perspective.

Speaking With the Boss's Authority

There are times when you will speak on the boss's behalf and need to speak with his or her authority. Be willing to remind people whom you represent. Often support personnel downplay their role with words like:

— *I was wondering if maybe you could...*

— *Here's what I want you to do...*

Instead, use a **PowerPhrase for Communicating With Your Boss's Authority,** such as:

- **Ms. Big has sent me to get the following files...**
- **I know Mr. Big's expectations. This is what must be done...**
- **Joe Important did not suggest that there would be any problem in obtaining your support on his behalf.**

When you speak on your boss's behalf, remind people you have their authority.

These phrases carry more impact when the boss has credentialed you his or herself. Some supervisors use

PowerPhrases to Credential Their Staff, such as:

- **When _____ opens her mouth my voice comes out.**
- **While I am away I expect you to regard what _____ says as if you heard it from me.**
- **She's the boss when I'm gone.**

If you need to be credentialed, ask your supervisor to use one of these expressions.

It is in your interest as well as your boss's interest that you assertively ask for what you need in a straightforward way. That is what your PowerPhrases at work are for.

 It's up to you. Ask for that raise you deserve. *How to Ask For a Raise: The Top Ten Dos, Don'ts and PowerPhrases for Getting Paid What You Deserve.* http://www.speakstrong.com/articles/ workplace-communication/howtoaskforaraise.html

CHAPTER 9

PowerPhrases® at Work: Communicating With Coworkers

Coworkers can be your allies… or your adversaries. Be sure to cultivate coworkers as allies at every level of the organization, from the janitor, to the mailroom, to the CEO.

Offer help and ask for help when you need it. For example, if you are making labels, ask yourself who else can use labels. Then offer:

• Joan, I'm making labels, do you want some too?

Ask:

• What can I do for you?

Say:

• I need your help.

These are all PowerPhrases.

Take an interest in your peers. Listen, listen, and listen. It is amazing to hear people go on and on without realizing that they haven't asked about the other person. Often it is to your advantage to allow that. You can learn a lot just listening and encouraging them to speak.

Here is what you don't want to say:

— *I'd like to get to know you. Let me tell you all about myself.*

— *Let me tell you about the week I had. It all started with…*

Cultivate coworkers as allies at every level of the organization.

Instead use a **PowerPhrase for Expressing Interest,** such as:

• There is so much I want to learn from you.

• Tell me what it's like for you around here.

• I'd like a chance to speak with you. When can we arrange that?

• Do you mind if I pick your brain?

• Can I take you to lunch?

Be sure to solicit support for your ideas from your colleagues to encourage buy-in. Rather than simply asking for support, GIVE them something. Use a **PowerPhrase for Soliciting Support for an Idea,** such as:

• Joan, I want to give you the first chance to review the XYZ proposal before the meeting. Your recommendations and support will help it in the approval process.

• I invite your involvement in the spring-loaded widget project in its early development when you can still help shape things. Your expertise can make a huge difference here.

Rather than simply asking for support, GIVE coworkers something.

People tend to support ideas and initiatives they had a role in creating.

Giving Feedback to Coworkers

We all like to look good in front of our employers, so give positive feedback in front of others, and corrective feedback in private. Question the urge to give corrective feedback before you do it. When someone suggests an idea and requests your feedback, avoid being a wet blanket and saying things like:

— *What's wrong with the way things are now?*

— *You're kidding, right?*

If that is your first impulse, reply with a **PowerPhrase to Buy Time to Consider an Idea,** such as:

- That's an interesting idea.
- I never thought of that.

When you do give feedback, consider the following.

1. Feedback Needs to Be Specific.

They need to be able to apply the ideas. Don't use vague words like:

— *Great job!*

— *You could have done a better job.*

Instead use a **PowerPhrase for Specific Feedback,** such as:

- I particularly like the way you did A. What I like most about how you did it is...
- A, B and C work well. Some suggestions I have for D, E and F are...

2. Feedback Needs to Be Solution Oriented.

If there are problems, focus on how they can be fixed. Instead of saying:

— *This is wrong and that is wrong and everything else is awful too.*

Use a **PowerPhrase for Offering Solutions in Feedback,** such as:

- One way to strengthen A is... Have you considered ... for B? C could be improved by...

3. Feedback Needs to Express Facts as Facts and Opinions as Opinions. Rather that passing a judgment like:

— *The exercises were useless.*

Communicate an experience like:

- I did not see the value in the exercises.

Feedback needs to be solution oriented.

4. Feedback Needs to Be Consistent.

If you wait to give feedback until there is a problem, people will resist. Be sure to tell people how much you appreciate positive things they do even if they are just "doing their job."

Use a **PowerPhrase for Consistent Feedback.**

• **I want to let you know how much I appreciate your ___ every day.**

• **Thanks for making my job easier by...**

• **I always appreciate the way you...**

• **Thank you for ___.**

Say it and walk away. If you glance back you will see their jaw drop open because chances are good they were expecting a "but" followed by everything they do wrong.

Consistently give positive feedback in addition to pointing out problem areas.

Power Pointer— Use the Power of Praise

When doing training for The Department of Defense, I had the group do an exercise that is recommended by Barbara Fielder in "Motivation in the Workplace." She gives everyone ten coins to put in their pocket. Then she has them circulate and acknowledge each other. Every time they acknowledge someone, they transfer a coin from one pocket to the other. The goal is to transfer all coins by the end of the day.

I gave this group five coins and three days to do the exercise in, but only a few did it. Finally I called an acknowledgement break. I told them they could not sit down until they had transferred all five coins. No one moved. It took several minutes of insisting until someone finally started the process.

The room transformed once the group finally got started. Hearts opened and people were delighted. Individuals who were at odds with each other acknowledged each other.

Try the ten-coin exercise and see what it does for you.

For most people, giving positive feedback is sufficiently rare that it is important to develop a system to make sure you do it.

Handling Interruptions

Do you hate it when people poke their heads in and say, "Got a minute?" What they are really asking is "Are you doing something that is more important than I am?" Ask *yourself* the same question.

To handle interruptions, use the three-step process for saying no. Begin with an acknowledgement of the request. Then briefly describe your situation. Finally, reaffirm the relationship.

Handling Interruptions Using the Three-Step Process for Saying No

When interrupted, ask yourself: what is the priority? Their request or what I am working on?

Acknowledge	Circumstance	Transform
Yes, I see what you are asking.	I have a 2:00 deadline.	I can talk with you after that.
I'd like to help.	5 minutes is all I have.	Will that help?
This would require my full attention.	I don't have it to give right now.	I believe you can handle it yourself.
I understand what you need.	Now is not a good time.	If you still need help tomorrow I might be able to fit it in.

If you find yourself complaining about someone who interrupts you, you know you need to use PowerPhrases to handle those interruptions.

PowerPhrases for Meetings

You have a chance to shine at meetings, as well as a chance to practice all of your positive office politics skills. For example, what do you do when someone expresses your idea and takes credit for it? Speak up. Don't let it pass, and don't say:

— Hey, that was my idea! You stole it!

Instead, use a **PowerPhrase for Taking Credit for Your Ideas,** such as:

- I believe that idea started with a comment I made earlier. I want to elaborate on my thinking.

- That is what I was referring to when I said… I am glad you like my idea, and I like the way you elaborated on it.

Later you can address the offender using the conflict model from Chapter 4. If it often happens that other people take credit for your ideas, ask someone:

- Is there something about the way I present my ideas that makes it hard to take them seriously?

There may be something about how you are expressing yourself that sabotages you.

When you have the floor and someone interrupts, ask yourself if you are being wordy and trying his or her patience. If not, use a **PowerPhrase to Handle Interrupters,** such as:

- Excuse me. I wasn't finished yet.

- I want to hear what you have to say as soon as I am done.

If someone is dominating the discussion, say:

- You have great ideas on the subject. Let's open the floor up for input from others.

- Since the agenda allows us only another ten minutes on this topic, we need to keep this moving. Please give us the condensed version and allow time for other comments before ending this discussion.

When you have the floor and someone interrupts, use a PowerPhrase to handle interrupters.

Sometimes you can simply say:

• There is only time for the short version, please.

Encouraging Participation

If you are leading the meeting, one of your responsibilities is to encourage input from members who may not speak without encouragement. Simply say:

• ___, what is your opinion on the subject?

If they do not offer an opinion, it is appropriate to ask again, by saying:

• **Your ideas do not need to be polished. We need to know what direction your thinking is taking.**

When there is a side conversation going on, it needs to be addressed. Use a **PowerPhrase for Addressing a Side Conversation,** such as:

When a side conversation goes on at a meeting, address it.

• **Please give Bill your full attention.**

• **When Bill finishes, I invite your comments.**

• **We all want to end this meeting on time, and that requires speaking one at a time.**

• **We have a lot of material to cover, and I'd rather not get off track. At the break let's get together, and this way I'll be able to give your concerns more individual attention.**

If someone is late, rather than reviewing what he or she missed, tell the offender:

• **Be sure to ask someone to catch you up on what was missed later.**

Address the issue of ongoing lateness later.

When issues are brought up that are not on the agenda, rather than addressing the inappropriate topic, use a **PowerPhrase for Maintaining the Agenda,** such as:

• That's an important topic. Please make sure that it gets on the agenda for a future meeting.

Meetings can be useful and meetings can be nightmares. PowerPhrases make the difference in which they are.

Handling Backstabbing Coworkers

Backstabbing is a common office practice. You can stop it. If you hear about someone talking about you behind your back, make your **CASE. Clarify** what you have heard, and **assert** yourself using the steps outlined in chapter 3. You can then **seek** solutions and **evaluate** them.

Use the Four Step Process to Assert Yourself with Backstabbers While Making Your Case

Problem	Impact: Thoughts/ Feelings/Effect	Request	Consequence
When I heard that you complained to others about the quality of my work...	I was devastated. I questioned our working relationship and began to wonder how safe it is to be open with you.	In the future, come to me directly if there is an issue.	I will do the same for you.
I confided in you, and I have reason to believe that you shared my secrets with others.	This can destroy our working relationship.	What can I do to ensure that my confidences are honored?	I will only confide in you if I feel secure.

Backstabbing is passive-aggressive. Address it.

Backstabbing is passive-aggressive, and needs to be addressed straightforwardly. Use the four step process to assert yourself clearly.

Dealing With Unsolicited Advice

When a coworker gives you unsolicited advice, again, make your **CASE**. Be sure you clarify their intent before asserting yourself. Then use some or all of the four-step model to assert yourself, followed by seeking solutions and evaluating them.

Dealing With Unsolicited Advice

Problem	Impact: Thoughts/ Feelings/Effect	Solution/ Request	Consequence
When you offer advice,	I get confused.	Please refrain from advising me unless I request it.	I will do the same for you.
When you tell me how to do my job,	I think you do not trust me.		

Enjoy the clarity that comes with PowerPhrases.

Communicate clearly and effectively with your coworkers and enjoy the clarity that comes with PowerPhrases.

How to Be the Assertive Manager Your Employees Want to Produce Results For: Management Skill Training for Effective Communication Management Skill Training tips to help managers assertively manage employees.
http://www.speakstrong.com/articles/
performance-management/assertive.html

CHAPTER 10

PowerPhrases® at Work: Magic Phrases for Managers

If you are a manager, you are the most important influence in the work life of your employees. That's huge... and it's true. As a manager, you impact the performance and morale of your employees more than any other factor. That is a great deal of responsibility. You do make a difference...whether you want to or not. That's why PowerPhrases for managers are essential.

Your success as a manager or supervisor begins at the interview. Hiring the right people is one of the most important things you can do. Know what questions to ask. There are many standard interview questions that are effective.

A good interview question addresses the job the applicant is applying for and how they would handle a specific situation.

- **Why do you want this job?**
- **What are your strengths?**
- **What are your weaknesses?**
- **What makes you the best candidate?**
- **Why should I hire you?**

Marlene Caroselli suggests a few more unusual questions.

- **Tell me about myself.** (Yes, you read it right. The purpose is to assess the candidate's judgment of character.)

- **If you were the president of this company, what is one new policy/plan/product you would initiate?**[8]

[8] Marlene Caroselli, *Hiring and Firing*, Mission, KS: SkillPath Publications 1993

A good interview question addresses the job the applicant is applying for and how they would handle a specific situation.

- What would you do to increase consumer widget awareness?

- When two managers insist that you give their projects priority, how do you handle it?

- What are you most proud about in your previous job?

- How do you solve problems?

- This job calls for... What is your experience in this?

- This job requires... Tell me about your success in this area.

- What would your previous staff/bosses say about you?

Use open-ended questions that draw the candidates out.

Marlene Caroselli also recommends that you use open-ended questions that start with...

- What...

- Explain...

- Describe...

- How would you...?

- In what ways...

- Under what circumstance do you...?

- If you could...

- Please cite some examples of...

- Tell me about...[9]

Avoid asking questions that can get you in legal problems. There are safe ways to get the information you require.

[9] Marlene Caroselli, *Hiring and Firing*, Mission KS: SkillPath Publications 1993

Instead of asking:

— *What kind of accent do you have?*

Ask:

• **Do you have legal verification of your right to work in this country?**

Instead of asking:

— *What's your native language?*

Ask:

• **What languages do you speak, read or write?**

Instead of asking:

— *Are you religious?*

Ask:

• **These are the hours, days and shifts that are to be worked. Is there anything that would interfere with your ability to work these hours?**

Instead of asking:

— *How old are you?*

Ask:

• **If we hire you, do you have proof of your age?**

Instead of asking:

— *Do you have kids?*

Ask:

• **Are you comfortable with our policy of not allowing personal phone calls at work?**

Instead of asking:

— *Does your disability keep you from being able to…?*

Ask:

• **Is there anything that keeps you from being able to…?**

Avoid asking questions that can get you in legal problems.

Other questions include:

- I see you worked at ___ from ___ to ___. Why did you choose that firm?

Be aware that many applicants supply false information. Probe to discover what is valid. The more specific and detailed your questions are, the more likely you are to uncover the facts.

Power Preparation

The PowerPhrases listed for interviews and terminations are not meant to replace legal advice. Be sure you clearly understand the laws of hiring and firing as well as your company's policies. Be certain that your words and actions conform to the Civil Rights Act of 1964, The American Disabilities Act of 1990 and the Equal Employment Opportunity Act of 1972.

When you turn down a potential applicant, be prepared to explain why.

End the interview by saying:

- What happens next is…
- You can expect to hear back by…

You probably do not enjoy turning down a potential applicant. When you do, be prepared to explain why. Be kind of course. The information may be helpful to them next time. If you can, say:

- It was a tough decision.
- We found someone with a few skills and a different kind of training that we need.

If there is something specific that disqualified them, let them know.

• **Next interview you have, I recommend that you...**

• **We felt you were under-prepared for the interview.**

People tell me they have been baffled about why they were not hired for numerous jobs, and were grateful when someone gave them useful feedback about why they were not selected.

Orienting New Employees

On the employee's first day, make a special effort to get them off to a great start. Be careful that your new employees don't get a message that sounds like:

— *Good luck!*

— *You're on your own.*

When orienting new employees, use positives to express company policy. Avoid saying:

— *Don't steal.*

— *Don't come to work looking scuzzy.*

New employees need a strong orientation to get them off to a good start.

Instead, talk about what you want rather than what you don't want. Use **PowerPhrases to Orient New Employees,** such as:

• **We expect our employees to safeguard company property from theft.**

• **We require our employees to dress according to the following dress code.**

Go on to orient new employees by saying:

• **The history, mission and goals of the department/company are...**

• **We are glad you are here!**

• **What questions do you have?**

• **Let me introduce you around. This is...**

- Your job responsibilities are...
- When you get stuck, here's what you do.
- When you need help, this is whom you turn to.

When giving employees assignments, whether they are new or old, be sure to follow the recommendations for delegation.

Delegation

Do you resist delegating or do it ineffectively? Delegation is a five-step process. Delegating consists of:

1. An optional opening,
2. A benefit to them,
3. A clear description of what is to be done,
4. A confirmation of understanding of the task, and
5. A confirmation of commitment.

There are PowerPhrases for each.

Make sure the person that you are delegating to knows what they can gain from taking the task on.

1. Opening

Here are the words to avoid:

— *You don't look busy. Will you...?*

— *I'm asking you to do this because I don't want to...*

— *I hate to ask you but...*

— *Sorry to bother you but...*

— *I was wondering if maybe you would...*

Instead use a **PowerPhrase Opener for Delegation,** such as:

- Although I am aware of how busy you are, I have a request...
- I would never ask you to do something I would not do myself...
- There is an opportunity here for you to...

• I'm asking you because I know I can trust you...

Then make sure they know what they can gain from taking the task on.

2. Benefit

Follow the request with a **PowerPhrase for Communicating a Benefit to Them**, such as:

• What this means to you is...

• This will help you by...

• If you do this for me I will...

• I'll make sure my boss knows how you made a difference when I really needed you.

3. Describe

Be sure the task description is clear. Avoid vague statements:

> — *I need this sometime.*

> — *Here. You figure it out.*

Instead, use a **PowerPhrase to Ensure a Clear Description,** such as:

• I need _____ by _____because_____.

• Here is what needs to happen...

• I have written out instructions. Let's go over them together.

• The deadline is ___, the quality specifications are ___ and the budget is ___. Of these three, the priority in this project is ___.

4. Confirm

Confirm their understanding of the task. Don't say:

> — *Do you have any questions?*

> — *Do you understand?*

*Be sure the
task description
is clear.*

Instead, ask open-ended questions, using a **PowerPhrase to Confirm Understanding**, such as:

- What did I leave out?
- What would you like reviewed?
- What will your first step be?
- Let me make sure my instructions are clear. What is your understanding of what I have told you?
- What questions do you have?
- What ideas do you have about...?
- What do you think about...?

You may think you are being perfectly clear, but often times what seems clear to you does not to them.

5. Commitment

Get a firm commitment before leaving the task to them.

Be sure to have a firm commitment before leaving the task to them. Use a **PowerPhrase for Getting Commitment,** such as:

- Can I count on you?
- When will you have that for me?

Put it all together into:

The Five-Step Process for Delegating

Combine phrases from the different categories to make your requests powerfully without being overbearing.

Opening	What's in It for Them	Clear Request	Confirm Understanding	Get Commitment
I would never delegate anything I wasn't willing to do myself.[10]	What this means for you is____.	I need ___ by ___ because___.	What did I leave out?	When will you have that?

[10] Mark Tower, *Dynamic Delegation*, Mission, KS: SkillPath Publications 199?

Opening	What's in It for Them	Clear Request	Confirm Understanding	Get Commitment
There is something important that needs to be done.	If you help us out here I will make sure my boss knows how you pitched in.	I have clear written instructions. I want to go over them with you.	What can I clarify?	Can we count on you for this?
I need your help…	If you do this for me I will…	My situation is… and I need…	What questions can I answer for you?	Will you do this for me?

The Four-Step Process for Delegating

The first steps can be combined. You can open with a statement that offers a benefit.

Opening — What's in It for Them	Clear Request	Confirm Understanding	Get Commitment
This is a critical task that must be done. It is not just busy work.[11]	What I need is… The deadline is… The budget is…	Let me make sure my instructions were clear. What is your understanding of the task?	Let's schedule the first follow-up session.
I have an opportunity for you that will help you learn how to…	This is the objective…, this is the means…, these are the boundaries…	How will you begin?	When will you begin?

Give the authority to your delegate and let others know that they have it.

In *Dynamic Delegation*, Mark Tower observes: "The delegator must keep what he or she wants to give up–responsibility. Conversely, he or she must give up what he or she wants to keep–authority."[12] Be sure to give the authority to your delegatee and let others know that they have it. Some phrases are listed in Chapter 8. Other **PowerPhrases to Credential Your Employees** are:

[11] Mark Tower, *Dynamic Delegation*, Mission KS: SkillPath Publications 1993
[12] Mark Tower, *Dynamic Delegation*, Mission KS: SkillPath Publications 1993

- ___ speaks for me.
- When ___ asks for something I expect you to give it to her.
- ___ is in charge of ___. Please give her your full cooperation.

When delegating, schedule follow-up sessions. At these sessions you can use a **PowerPhrase for Following-Up on Delegation**, such as:

- Please give us an update of your progress.
- Is the project running on schedule?
- Is everything within budget?
- Are the quality specifications being met?
- What can I do to support your work?

Of course you may not like the answers that you get. You might find that you need to coach.

Proper delegation takes more time up front and saves time in the long run.

Power Pointer— Coaching Is a Skill

My son David is a computer genius, but for many years he was not skilled at showing me how to do things so I could do them myself. David would sit at the computer with his fingers flying over the keyboard, speaking in a "foreign language." When I asked for help with the same issue again, he complained, "Mom, I already showed you how to do that!" He showed me, but he did not empower me to be self-sufficient.

This changed after David worked for years at a help desk. He had a much better idea of what questions I had, and he patiently took me through the steps at my own pace so I could internalize them. He asked questions to verify my understanding. The different approach took more time up front, but ultimately saved time for us both.

Coaching Employees

Coaching through problems is a matter of making your CASE. (1) **Clarify** their position, (2) **Assert** yourself, (3) **Seek** solutions, (4) **Evaluate** options and create agreements.

1. Clarify Their Position

When you clarify their position, ask questions and LISTEN. Find things to acknowledge in their work.

Make sure your words do not imply:

— *I'll do the talking around here.*

— *Why should I listen to you?*

— *You idiot! You blew it again!*

Instead, use a **PowerPhrase to Solicit Their Perspective,** such as:

When you clarify their position, ask questions and LISTEN.

• **What do you think of your performance?**

• **Do you understand why there is a problem with your behavior?**

• **How do you see the problem?**

Listen carefully and acknowledge what they say before explaining your perspective.

2. Assert Your Position

Do not limit your comments to where they fall short of expectations. Instead, begin with mention of whatever positives you can comfortably acknowledge. Use a PowerPhrase for **Acknowledging Their Work,** such as:

• I like the way you did...

• This work shows a lot of attention to detail...

• I see progress with...

• Your... in the face of... means a lot.[13]

[13] Donald Weiss, *Why Didn't I Say That?* New York: Amacom Publications, 1994

Follow with a description of the problem. Again, be specific and unless it is obvious, describe why it is a problem. Avoid vague statements such as:

— *You could have done a better job.*

— *It's not good enough.*

— *This is terrible.*

Instead, use a **PowerPhrase for Describing the Problem,** such as:

- **The problem with _____ is that ____, which results in ___. (Ex: The problem with this report is that it lacks detail, which leaves questions in the reader's mind.)**

- **What doesn't work so well is ___ because ___. (What doesn't work is the summary because new information is introduced which causes confusion.)**

- **I see a problem with ____ that could cause ____.**

Remember your goal is to educate and inform.

3. Seek Solutions

Put most of your coaching effort into discussing solutions. Talk about what you want more than what you don't want. If you want to encourage them to solve more of their own problems, avoid dictating solutions. Encourage them to develop a habit of thinking for themselves. The best solutions are the ones they come up with on their own—or that you come up with together.

Avoid dictatorial phrases such as:

— *Do it this way.*

— *I don't know what to do—you figure it out.*

— *Any idiot knows that the best way to do it is…*

Instead, use a **PowerPhrase for Creating Solutions,** such as:

The best solutions are the ones employees come up with on their own or that you come up with together.

- Let's look at what works and figure out what we can learn to deal with the problems.
- My recommendation is… What do you think?
- How do you plan to proceed?
- What do you intend to do about the problem?
- Let's look for solutions together.
- Here is another way of doing it.
- What do you suggest that we do to keep this from happening again?
- What is your plan to upgrade quality?
- What would it take to ___ (ex. get you on time with deadlines)?

Keep the attitude of working together.

4. Evaluate Options and Create Agreements

When you evaluate solutions, remember: your solutions need to be realistic in order to be effective. If someone has a swearing problem, a zero-tolerance policy is unlikely to work. They might mean well, but the first time they drop something on their toe, watch them let it fly! Use a **PowerPhrase to Evaluate Options,** such as:

- Does this option solve the problem?
- Do you believe that you can comply with this option?
- Is there any way this option can be improved?
- Is this an option that you will be able to commit to in writing?

Be sure to get the commitment in writing, and arrange for your follow up meeting.

You can use this structure for coaching in performance reviews as well.

Solutions need to be realistic in order to be effective.

The Performance Review

Begin the review by making the employee as comfortable as you can. Start with a welcome and an overview of the procedure.

- As you know, this is an opportunity for us to share information about your job, to clarify objectives and to see how things are going for you.

- Then we can discuss growth.

- I will put my calls on hold so we won't be interrupted.

Then go directly into reviewing goals and reviewing performance.

- Let us compare notes on your top three goals and means to achieve them.

- Please give me examples.

- What will it take for you to meet your next quarter's goals?

Where performance needs to be improved, refer back to the section about coaching employees as well as the phrases below.

Begin a performance review by making the employee as comfortable as you can; then go directly into reviewing goals and reviewing performance.

PowerPhrases for Improving Performance

--Acknowledge	Describe Problem	Find Solutions
I like the way you ___.	What does not work as well is ___ because___ results in ___.	Let's look for solutions together.
I see progress with ___.	What I see that still needs work is...	How do you plan to proceed?
This work shows a lot of attention to detail.	Until the last page.	How can you add detail to the last page?
Generally I am very pleased with your work.	One area needs work. Perhaps I haven't made it clear that you are responsible for... and some problems are...	How can I help you succeed?
While I have seen improvement in quality,	when you...(submit the work for a big project three days late), the effect is...(we all have to wait before revisions can be made). We feel... (frustrated and angry).	Let's talk about time management.

When you must refuse a request from an employee, ACT.

PowerPhrases for Refusing Requests From Employees

Employees will ask for things we do not want to or cannot give them. When you must refuse a request from an employee, use the ACT formula for saying no from Chapter 3. Acknowledge the request, briefly explain circumstances of why you are unable to grant it, and transform the refusal into a positive. Here is the formula applied to an employee request.

Acknowledge	Circumstances	Transform
I understand you are asking for…	I am unable to fulfill your request because…	What I can do is…
I am delighted with the work you have been doing the few months you have been here.	You haven't been here very long and the policy does not allow me to even consider a raise before the first year.	Let's review your performance and set goals so that when the first year mark comes, you will get the largest increase possible.
I appreciate your need for more money.	Right now your performance does not merit consideration for a raise.	Let's review the two areas where improvement would indicate a raise in the future.
We love having you here.	We simply cannot afford a raise at this time.	You have a great future here and I hope you will stay until things turn around in this company.
I am aware that the computer that is assigned to you is slow.	Based on the amount of computer work you do, I cannot justify the expense of a new one.	If you can show me something I am overlooking I am happy to reconsider.
I agree that improvements in the warehouse are needed.	Funding only allows for a few.	Let's get some representatives to make suggestions on which ones they will be.

When an employee must be discharged for non-performance reasons, the words are never easy to find.

Termination

When the appropriate coaching sessions fail to bring positive results and standards have not been met, or when an employee must be discharged for non-performance related reasons, the words are never easy to find.

Power Questions to Ask Yourself Prior to Termination

In Hiring and Firing by Marlene Caroselli, E.D., Marlene quotes Stephen M. Karas, First Vice President, Manager of Major Buildings Division for Security Pacific Bank as saying that prior to terminating anyone, he asks himself the following questions:

• Did I do everything I could to assist this person?

• Did I communicate properly?

• Did he or she have all the tools necessary to do the job?

It is tempting to assume that the employee who did not work out is the problem. Powerful managers look to themselves to see what is to be learned from the experience.

Usually the employee already suspects the inevitable. Your job is to make it as quick and clean as possible, and to preserve as much of the other person's dignity as you can. Begin with an opening, explain the situation in a minimum of detail, and reaffirm the other person.

Before termination the employee usually already suspects the inevitable.

The Three-Step Process for Termination

Opening	Explain	Reaffirm
I suspect you have guessed what this meeting is about.	In our prior meetings we have outlined the standards you must meet to stay on with us and they have not been met.	HR has a few leads for other jobs.
I am forced to terminate your employment.	Despite warnings your performance level has not reached acceptable levels.	I hope you find work that suits you in the future.
I feel sad to tell you,	budget cutbacks have forced the elimination of your position.	I understand that Extraordinary Widgets is looking for people with your qualifications.
I have bad news for you.	Your employment here is terminated.	How can I help you pull resources together?
We have come to a final decision regarding your employment.	The reasons are as follows…	Personnel will discuss your final pay and collect your office keys.
I have to terminate your employment effective immediately.	You have been told what is expected and been given written warnings, but the expectations have not been met.	I wish this could have been resolved otherwise.

Make termination as clean and quick as possible to protect the employee's dignity.

Use statements that encourage the terminated employee toward action.

Power Thinking— Effective Management Requires Powerful Decision Making

It might comfort you to know that while immediately following a firing, 75% described the firing as the "worst thing that ever happened to them"; one year later the vast majority describes it as "the best thing that ever happened."[14] Of course, as a supervisor, your first loyalty is to the organization. Many times that requires you to be firm.

Termination is probably the most difficult part of managing. As with any other aspect of management, it requires assertively saying what you mean, meaning what you say without being mean when you say it.

Good management requires good PowerPhrases. From the initial interview and throughout your role as manager, use PowerPhrases to make yourself more effective. In the next chapter you will learn how to create your own.

Good management requires good PowerPhrases.

[14] Marlene Caroselli, Hiring and Firing, Mission, KS: SkillPath Publications 1993

Check out my *PowerPhrase Tutorial* at:
http://www.speakstrong.com/tutorial/index.html

CHAPTER 11

Now It's Your Turn—Create Your Own PowerPhrases®

What would life be like if you could say what you wanted whenever you wanted? Can you imagine the freedom of always being able to say what you mean, and not having to worry about anyone ever taking offense? Wouldn't it be great if the honest expression of whatever you thought and felt always got good results?

In my fantasy world the raw truth works every time, but in the real world, it is in your best interests to edit. You discovered the need to edit early in life. Speaking your mind would backfire! Unfortunately you probably took self-editing too far. You probably did not just edit your words. My guess is that you also edited what you were willing to become conscious of thinking and feeling.

What would life be like if you could say what you wanted whenever you wanted?

Read that paragraph again, because it is huge in its implications for PowerPhrases. It is also huge in implications for your life.

To create your own effective PowerPhrases you first must become aware of what it is that you would say in the perfect world I described above. Then edit your words to get the results you desire.

You have been editing your thoughts and feelings for so long, that it will take work to uncover the truth now. An excellent way is through writing.

What would you really like to say to your boss if you

knew there would be no negative repercussions? Would you ever say something like this?

> — *Listen, you narcissist—this conversation is getting us nowhere. They might pay you three times what they pay me to bore the people that work for you with your empty accomplishments, but I happen to take my job seriously and I have more important things to do than to hear you brag about nothing. You are so pitiful, and if I didn't feel like puking I might feel sorry for you.*

Does it feel good to express it on paper? (Do be careful about what you do with that paper.) After getting clarity about your thoughts, feelings and what you would LIKE to say in a situation like this, you will find it easier to say:

- **I prefer that we stay on the subject of our product line. Like you, I have a number of deadlines to meet.**

What would you really like to say if you knew there would be no negative repercussions?

Power Pointer— Finding Your Inner Voice Can Take Time

A song I wrote has the following lyrics:

So much of who I am is an illusion.

An act of who I think I'm s'pozed to be.

All this make-believe creates confusion.

I don't know what's real inside of me.

One of the hardest parts of PowerPhrases can be quieting your inner-editor long enough to learn what you would really like to say.

Eight Steps to Your Own PowerPhrases

Create Your Own PowerPhrases Using the Following Eight Steps:

1. Write a freeform letter saying what you would if my perfect world of free expression was a real one.
2. Review the letter for the essential message.
3. Determine what results you seek by communicating.
4. Start writing what you want to actually say, considering the results you want.
5. Ask yourself the PowerPhrase questions from the end of chapter 1. (See the review later in this chapter.)
6. Edit for Poison Phrases from chapter 2.
7. Run it by a friend.
8. Take a deep breath, use your pass the butter voice (described in the introduction) and express yourself.

Step One: Tools for Your Freeform Letter

Writing your freeform letter is a *simple* process; however, it is not an *easy* process. You will think it takes an eternity to discover what you really want to say. Some of your thoughts will contradict others. The truth in your heart is multi-dimensional. What makes sense at one level does not make sense at another. Do not be in too big of a hurry to make it all add up. Take your time. Allow your inner truths to emerge.

The truth in your heart is multi-dimensional. Allow your inner truths to emerge.

Ask yourself the following questions:

1. What might I be angry about?
2. What hurts?
3. What am I afraid of?
4. What do I regret?
5. Is there something I feel shame about that I do

not want to admit to myself or the other person?

6. What do I want to have happen?

7. What do I want this person to know?

Do not lie to yourself. This is simply information to be considered in discovering what it is you need and want, as well as in understanding how to get it. Now move to step 2.

Step 2: Review the Letter for the Essential Message

Once you have expressed yourself on paper, notice themes in your thoughts and feelings. Some of the things you write will seem insignificant. Other words will have a clear ring of truth. Note what ideas repeat. Notice what touches you the most emotionally when you review it. Also notice if you feel resistant to some of what you write. If you feel resistance to your words, ask yourself why. Is there something that you do not want to admit to yourself? Is there something that you do not want to have to tell someone else? Don't worry—you do not have to act on or express everything you think and feel—in fact I recommend that you don't! Do examine your responses to what you wrote to understand yourself better.

If you feel resistance to your words, ask yourself why.

Step 3: Determine What Results You Seek by Communicating.

The power of a communication is best measured by the result it obtains. Be clear of your intention before you formulate your PowerPhrases. Ask yourself:

1. Are you speaking to unburden yourself?

2. Are you speaking to get the other person to stop doing something?

3. Are you speaking to get the other person to start doing something?

4. Are you speaking to create a bond?

5. Are you speaking to relay information?

6. Are you speaking to punish or extract revenge? (Not recommended.)

The words you choose will depend on the result you want to accomplish.

Step 4: Start Writing What You Want to Actually Say, Keeping the Results in Mind.

Refer back to your intention and your freeform writing as you begin to formulate your own PowerPhrases. Also refer to the chapters that relate most to your issue. If you need to say no, refer to the **ACT** formula. If the issue is a conflict, make your **CASE**. Refer to the PowerPhrases I recommend, and create your own.

Step 5: Ask Yourself the PowerPhrase Questions From the End of Chapter One

Apply the PowerPhrase questions at the end of Chapter One to your writing. They are summarized below.

Apply the PowerPhrase Principles to every word you use.

A. Is it short? Eliminate all unnecessary words.

B. Is it specific? Can you find more powerful words?

C. Although you are editing your raw thoughts, does it say what you truly mean?

D. Are you certain that you are ready to back up your words with action?

E. Are there trigger words, accusations, and remarks that do not consider the self-esteem of your listener?

Step 6: Edit for Poison Phrases

Review your words one more time to make certain that there are no Poison Phrases listed in Chapter 2.

Step 7: Run It by a Friend

You are probably too involved with your own situation to be objective. Try your communication out on a friend. Ask your friend how he or she would respond if they received a communication like the one you prepared.

Step 8: Take a Deep Breath, Use Your Pass the Butter Voice and Express Yourself.

You can do it! Say what you mean, mean what you say, and do not be mean when you say it.

Be aware that if you are speaking more powerfully than usual, your listener will not necessarily appreciate it. If someone is used to being able to get whatever he or she wants from you, they may not be pleased when you express yourself strongly. Even if people are accustomed to an aggressive behavior from you, they may resist calm assertiveness. A negative reaction does not imply you were wrong to speak. The ultimate test of that is how you feel about it.

Your listener will not always appreciate your new-found strength of communication.

PowerPhrases of Appreciation

PowerPhrases are not only for telling people what they need to change or what is not working. PowerPhrases are important to express the positives as well. When you review your freeform writing, pick out the words of appreciation that you find and be sure to express them as well. Below are a few of mine:

- Bob, with all the people in the world that you could be spending your life with, thank you for choosing me.

- David, you are the best thing that ever happened to me.

- Harriet, I am so glad that my Dad found you.

- Cindi, your zest for life increases mine.

- Bill, your unconditional friendship gives me a much needed refuge.

- Andy, thanks for your acceptance of me wherever I am at any time.

Now that you have the steps, start expressing yourself in such a way that others find out who you really are.

PowerPhrases are not only for telling people what they need to change or what is not working. PowerPhrases are important to express the positives as well.

217

Improve the power of your emails with: *How to Write Strong Subject Lines in Your E-mails: Top ten dos and don'ts of how to use subject lines more effectively.*
http://www.speakstrong.com/articles/email/
howtowritestrongsubjectlinesinyouremails.html

CHAPTER 12

Perfect PowerPhrases® for Effective Email

It's quick and it's easy. It can get you immediate results and it can get you into immediate trouble. Because of the speed of emails, you may send them hastily and without careful thought or review. Sloppy communication via email carries even more risk than it does in face-to-face communication. Emails create a written record, and you cannot see the reaction to know if there is confusion. PowerPhrases are even more important in email than they are in face-to-face conversation.

Like PowerPhrases, Effective Emails Are Brief

Stick to simple words, short phrases and paragraphs consisting of 1-3 short sentences. Don't require your recipient to think much, interpret long sentences or read big sections of text. If you ramble in emails, it can be more destructive to your message than if you ramble in conversation, because you have no control over what people do with your emails. In conversation, any word that does not add to the impact of your message when you speak detracts from it. In email, if you are wordy, you risk not being "heard" at all. People often scan emails to get a sense of the message. Too many words can bury the message. It also is common for people to review all new emails at once and mark longer ones for later reading... running a risk that your email will never get read at all.

PowerPhrases are even more important in emails than they are in face-to-face communication.

219

Ensure your message is received by making your emails as succinct as possible. Avoid wordiness such as:

— *I don't know if you heard about the details of the meeting that was held last Thursday. We raised a lot of important issues that concerned many of us. I wish you could have been there, but I understand you were busy. In case you do not have a copy of the minutes I am sending you one so you can offer your input. I know you're busy, but if you could…*

Instead, use a **PowerPhrase for Email Brevity** such as:

• **We missed you at the meeting. I am enclosing a copy of the minutes for your comment. Please review and forward your comments regarding item three by Friday.**

Keep emails succinct, but include a short relationship remark to avoid sounding abrupt.

This makes your message quick, easy to understand… and likely to be read. An excellent habit is to cut your first email draft in half before you send.

Take notice that although the above message is brief and focused, it does include a relationship remark—a single phrase whose purpose is to reinforce the relationship.

The Value of an Email Relationship Remark

In your attempt to keep your emails brief, avoid making them so brief that you sound abrupt. Emails lack non-verbal communication to reinforce the relationship, so use a brief phrase to highlight good will.

Some **PowerPhrases to Reinforce the Relationship in Emails** are:

• **We missed you at the meeting.**

• **I was glad to hear from you.**

• **I hope you enjoyed your trip.**

• **Thanks for your input.**

The best remarks are ones that are specific enough to

the person you are speaking to that they know you are paying attention to them.

Effective Emails Are Specific: Choose Your Words with Precision

Josh had fixed Larissa's software problems the week before and was wondering if everything was working properly. He emailed her asking:

— *Are you having any problems?*

When Larissa answered...

— *Thanks for asking. I have been concerned about my husband lately. He's had some health problems and...*

...Josh decided he should have been more specific.

The more specific your email, the more effective it will be. Include who, what, when, where and why, avoiding all vague words. You may choose to organize your email that way.

The more specific your email is, the more effective it will be.

• **Who: All senior managers**

• **What: Mandatory Compliance Update**

• **When: Thursday June 30th, 10:00–10:15**

• **Where: Boardroom**

• **Why: To ensure all new regulations are understood prior to inspections**

This format will reduce your risk of omitting important information. Specifics can save you time on follow-up emails, and specifics can eliminate error.

Even with a structure such as this one, ask yourself what information they might still require. For example, is there more than one boardroom? Each comment must be reviewed from the perspective of all recipients. Before you hit send, ask yourself the following two questions:

1. Is there any information I left out?

2. Are any of the words subject to an inaccurate interpretation?

In the example, does everyone know who is regarded as a senior manager? Are other members of their team invited or expected to attend? Be particularly aware of vague words such as:

— *Soon*

— *Quick*

— *Good*

— *Bad*

Words like:

• **By Thursday noon**

• **Under five minutes**

• **Profitable**

• **Inaccurate**

Avoid hints or any assumptions of understanding.

are less open to interpretation.

Avoid hints or any assumptions of understanding. When you choose the most precise word you save time and confusion.

Use Specific Headers to Increase Clarity

Be specific right from the beginning. Make the subject header so specific that even if the recipient never opens the email, they still get information. For example, instead of a subject line that says

— *Company picnic*

Say:

• **Company picnic June 22, respond by June 13th.**

The recipient knows at a glance what the email is about, and what action is required.

A Creative Header Succeeded Where All Else Failed

Sometimes subject headers that are interesting and compelling will get results when nothing else will. Cindi was getting no response to her emails to a coworker until she changed the subject line to say:

- Free beer

The email had nothing to do with beer, but the subject header did the job...the recipient opened the message and responded. Usually being specific and accurate in your header will be your best bet; however, when all else fails, go creative!

Effective Emails Are Results Oriented

Create Focus by Limiting Content of Your Emails

If you limit your email to one topic, it will add to the topic's impact. It is often better to send several emails than to load a single email with numerous unrelated topics. When separate topics are addressed in separate emails, the recipient knows they need to respond to each one.

Increase Clarity by Formatting

If you must include multiple topics in a single email, or if you have several points regarding a single topic, limit each paragraph to one topic and:

1. Give each a separate header and/or
2. Number or bullet each separate item.

"Jennifer" sent me an email that contained five questions listed numerically. After I responded, she marveled that she had asked five questions and I gave her five answers. I give Jennifer the credit for that, because

If you limit your emails to one topic, it adds to the topic's impact.

223

questions were enumerated. It was obvious what she wanted from me. Make it obvious to others what you are asking for, and easy for them to give it to you.

PowerPhrases Are Focused

Before you write, know what action you want your recipients to take. Answer important questions for the recipient in the first two sentences of your email. Your recipient wants to know immediately,

1. **Who you are**

2. **What do you want them to do?** And

3. **What's in it for them.**

When available, include "Call to Action" links to make it easy for them to comply.

Before you write, know what actions you want the recipients to take.

Handling Emotions on Emails

I heard a tale of a college student who told his colleagues he had asked his girlfriend to marry him. When his buddies asked what her response was, he replied:

— *I don't know. She hasn't answered my emails yet.*

Can you imagine the disappointment of their future grandchildren asking to hear the tale of how he popped the question? When it comes to handling sensitive topics and emotional issues via email, the best approach is not to.

Emotional topics and emails do not mix well. Meanings can be quickly misinterpreted.

When emotions get triggered, it is the time to leave your desk and speak to the person personally. At the very least, pick up the phone to speak directly. The reasons for this are:

1. If there are tensions, emails create a record that you might prefer they did not have. (If you in fact do want a record and you choose to discuss a sensitive issue via email despite the pitfalls, run your emails past a neutral party before you hit send.)

2. There is a greater chance of misunderstanding over email since there is not the face-to-face interaction to discern their response.

If someone brings up an issue that is sensitive via email, use a **PowerPhrase to Invite Direct Communication** such as:

- **This issue is too important to discuss over email. When can we meet?**

- **I want to be certain we understand each other. Let's continue this discussion face-to-face.**

- **My policy is to refrain from discussing sensitive issues by email. That's why I'm here. Is this a good time?**

Always question whether email is the best way to communicate, and be particularly careful when emotions are involved.

When emails get emotional, arrange to speak face-to-face.

A Few Words about Spelling and Grammar

I received an email asking a question about communication that contained multiple grammar errors. I admit I assumed the author was not well-educated until I realized English was her second language. It is unfortunate that we come to such inaccurate conclusions, but the fact is that we do when all we have to go on is words on a page. Therefore, take the time to correct spelling and grammar. Avoid all caps, and avoid all lower case. Do not allow errors to weaken the impact of your words.

If in Doubt, Ask.
Powerful Clarification Through Email

Information is missing in email that is available in face-to-face communication. That means it is imperative to clarify your understanding. If in doubt of meaning, ask. You cannot clarify too much. Keep your clarifications powerful.

Use **PowerPhrases for Email Clarification** such as:

You cannot clarify too much.

- **This is what I understand from your email. Is my understanding correct?**

- **Based on your previous email I intend to ___. Is that what you want me to do?**

Because the words are all the information you have with email, be even more aware of possible assumptions than you are in other forms of communication.

Pros and Cons of Email

Many of us love email because it is quick and easy. It is a comfortable way for the timid to interact and a rapid way for the hurried to correspond. Like most things in life, if used properly it can be an asset. If misused it can be a liability. A few well placed PowerPhrases can make the difference.

It's the way you knew the world should be.
Watch Meryl Runion's *A World of Truth* online.
http://www.speakstrong.com/worldoftruth.html

CHAPTER 13

The Truth about Truth, Persuasion and PowerPhrases®

Are you in love? If so, have I got a website for you! Go to calculator.com and look for the love calculator. When you click on it, it will ask you to enter your name and the name of your beloved to discover your chances of success. Before you hit enter, you have two options...

1. Tell the truth, and
2. Lie a little.

Why would anyone ask a question and ask for the answer to be a lie?

In fact we do it all the time. Most men have discovered that when their wives ask if their outfit makes them look fat, they don't really want to know. Many employees have discovered that when their boss asks for questions about the new initiative, they are really looking for agreement. Usually the question "How are you" is not a genuine inquiry into your well-being. You may say you want the truth when you really don't.

You may say you want the truth when you really don't.

What Is Truth?

What is truth? There's a question we can argue for a millennium. My purpose in raising this abstract topic is not to give the authoritative answer to what truth is, but to provide definitions of what I mean when I speak of telling the simple truth.

I make a distinction between personal truth and absolute truth. There are as many interpretations of the truth about anything as there are people who describe it. All you have to do is talk to more than one witness to an accident to discover that. There is an absolute truth of what happened that exists independent of how people perceive it. Then there are numerous versions of the truth, which include everyone's sincere assessment of what happened based on their personal perception. This is a collection of personal truths. Unfortunately, in determining the absolute truth of the accident, you are dependent on personal truth to put the picture together as objectively as possible. Even more unfortunate is that attempts to understand the absolute truth of an event are sometimes obscured by those who deliberately lie, and rather than telling their personal truth, they tell personal falsehood.

Don't wait for absolute certainty to speak up.

If I believe I had a green light and I say so, I am telling my personal truth: the truth as I know it. If a video camera later shows the light was red, it does not prove that I was lying, or even that I wasn't speaking the truth. It proves that the personal truth I told was likely not closely aligned with the absolute truth of the event. I was telling the truth, and was shown to be wrong.

That is different than if I deliberately lied about the color of the light.

The reason why this discussion is vital is that many people remain silent because they know that their personal truth is inherently limited. However, if you do not tell your personal truth to the best of your ability because you are afraid of error, those who willingly lie are given a free reign. Not only is absolute certainty not required to merit speaking up, there are compelling reasons to speak with whatever certainty you can muster. By speaking, you can discover the limitations—and accuracies—

of your personal truth. By speaking, others who have similar perceptions are also inspired to speak. By speaking, those who deliberately lie are put on notice that their assertions will not go unchallenged.

For the sake of clarity, when I speak of the simple truth, I am referring to your personal best efforts to speak accurately. When I speak of absolute truth, I am referring the truth that exists independent of anyone's perception of it.

Why We Lie: Eight Myths about Telling the Truth

There are many reasons why people avoid the truth and even lie. Some common barriers to truth telling are listed below. Fallacies of these barriers are discussed later in the chapter.

1. **Misplaced respect for authority.** Marie worked for a decorator. When her boss told her to cut the fabric for draperies, she knew the instructions were incorrect. She followed them anyway, ruining the fabric at great expense, and delaying the project by several months. Marie believed she was doing the right thing, because "the boss is the boss."

2. **Fear of negative consequences.** One of my newsletter subscribers spoke up brilliantly about an abusive manager…and lost her job. In the investigation of her charges, none of her coworkers would back her up due to fear.

3. **Not wanting to offend.** I get inquiries every week from managers who do not speak up about poor performance from their staff. While reading the detail of completely inappropriate behavior I anticipate the inevitable closing of: "S/he is so sensitive I don't want to hurt her/his feelings."

4. **Avoidance.** My late husband was paralyzed by fear of cancer. By not allowing a discussion he could avoid facing what he feared was true.

You can always find a reason to avoid the truth.

5. **Habit.** I first learned my parents were having marital difficulties the day they told me they were getting divorced. Keeping key issues silent was a family pattern which I learned and practiced until it became too costly.

6. **No one else is saying anything.** If no one else is saying anything, why should I? For example, it is common for managers to do a whitewash about poor performance on evaluations to avoid conflict, making it more difficult for subsequent managers to speak accurately.

7. **Self doubt.** Since it is impossible to know everything, it is easy to question your own understanding, especially if you are being told you're wrong. When I suspected my husband had cancer, I doubted myself in the face of his stated certainty that he did not have cancer.

8. **Don't know how.** Many people have the words to be passive, aggressive or passive aggressive, and don't know what words to use to be clear, direct, and kind.

There is a payoff—and a price—for silence.

A Case for Speaking Strong: Challenging the Myths

Certainly there is a payoff for silence—and there also is a price for silence. Usually the payoff is short-term and the price is long-term. Let's look at the credibility of each reason we use for not speaking the simple truth.

1. **Misplaced respect for authority:** History is full of failed efforts because the leaders were insulated from fact by yes-sayers. Respect for authority means having the respect to tell the truth. PowerPhrases can help you speak the truth in a manner that honors authority. In the example given about the interior decorator who gave inaccurate instructions, chances are the decorator would have preferred to have her directive challenged than have the draperies ruined by blind compliance.

2. **Fear of negative consequences:** This can be a legitimate concern which is why you must speak smart when you SpeakStrong. Assess the risks before speaking. When you assess the risks, consider the risks of NOT speaking as well as the risks of speaking. Some risks are: 1) Self-censorship can be physiologically damaging over an extended period of time. 2) When you don't speak up, you perpetuate an error or injustice. 3) While silence may prove more convenient short-term, ultimately the truth has a way of catching up with you. One of my favorite examples of this is the tale of John Olson who lost his job at Merrill Lynch for refusing to give Enron a buy-rating. Olson's commitment to the truth cost him his job, but he prevailed when truth prevailed.

When you choose to speak despite risks involved, speak with caution. The Government Accountability Project supports whistleblowers at a site called whistleblowers.com. They offer cautions before speaking out that can be useful in any industry or environment. (Guidelines are posted at http://www.whistleblower.org/article.php?did=33&scid=72)

Don't trick yourself into staying silent when the truth needs to be told.

3. **Not wanting to offend:** The irony of this argument against speaking up is that silence can cause resentment to build and damage relationships. I hear stories weekly from subscribers who discover that speaking up heals relationships that silence has damaged. Another problem with this argument is that it can make you vulnerable to people who will take advantage of your kindness to be able to get away with inappropriate behavior. Also, this reason can be used as an excuse. Often when I hear this reason given, the real issue is a desire to avoid conflict.

4. **Avoidance:** If you deny the truth it doesn't go away. There is a saying, "the best way out is though." While it is painful to address unwelcome reality, the only way to deal successfully with life is

to face the truth about what is. I believe had my late husband done this, he might be alive today.

5. **Habit:** Your habits are often invisible to you. Your habits are so automatic that you may not even know you are practicing them. The first step in changing any behavior is to become conscious of that behavior. Ask yourself, what are your habits about speaking out? Habits that do not serve you can be changed by consistent, persistent study, practice and evaluation. (A PowerPhrase a Week Newsletter, www.speakstrong.com, is popular because it helps develop new behaviors one week at a time.)

6. **No one else is saying anything:** There is a dangerous tendency to go with the status quo. A look at history tells you that mass consensus and opinion is not a good indicator of healthy behavior. If no one else is saying anything, it does not mean there isn't something that needs to be said. Countless injustices and falsehoods are perpetuated due to this reason. While the perpetuators of injustice and falsehoods are certainly responsible for their misinformation, if you are aware of lies and do not challenge them you are a co-conspirators. Challenging consensus can be a risk because the messenger is sometimes blamed for telling an unpopular truth. Then again, the person who dares to speak up often becomes the hero of those who were not willing to, and they make it safer for others to follow.

7. **Self doubt:** You do not need to have absolute certainty to SpeakStrong. You do need to give your best efforts at describing the truth. You are not expected to know absolute truth. The best you can do is to tell your personal truth...what your knowledge, perception and experience tells you is true. That is one thing you can be certain of. One dictionary definition of truth is sincerity and integrity. When you speak with sincerity and integrity, it inspires the same in others. That opens both of your perceptions to greater understanding.

The first step in changing any behavior is to become conscious of that behavior.

8. **Don't know how:** This is why PowerPhrases are imperative. My experience tells me that when people don't have the words to speak, they usually remain silent. Having the words makes all the difference.

Examine the reasons you give for not speaking truthfully and see if you are taking a short-term solution that will create a long-term problem.

Are there ever times when telling a deliberate lie is appropriate? I believe so, but they are rare. These are explored next.

Set Your "Default Mode" to Truth

There are specific circumstances when a lie may be appropriate. Otherwise, let truth win by default.

It may be appropriate to lie when there is nothing to be gained to offset the damage of telling an unpleasant truth. For example, there was nothing to be gained by my telling a long-term renter I thought the carpeting she selected was ugly.

Question any situation you are in that makes it difficult to tell the truth.

It may be appropriate to lie when dealing with unscrupulous people who will use the truth against you in an unfair way, such as when dealing with criminals.

However, if lying is not a singular event in your life, or you regularly are unable to speak the simple truth, reevaluate your assessment of the situation and reevaluate the situation itself. As "they" say, that ain't no way to live.

Persuasion and Propaganda

When you tell the truth, use persuasion rather than propaganda. Persuasion uses reasoning and argument to establish the truth of a position to induce a change. Propaganda uses opinions, images, and one-sided argument to spread the adoption of an idea regardless of its truth. Propaganda works best when reasoning is not engaged. Propaganda is designed to abort discussion.

Power Pointer— Propaganda versus Persuasion

Recently I had a conversation with a couple who have very different views from my own. I thought it would be an opportunity for me to understand their thinking. It wasn't. There was no reasoning, only opinion. For example, when I expressed my concerns about the possible reinstatement of the draft, they said, "That will never happen." When I asked why, they replied, "It just won't." I said I had information that led me to believe that it could, to which they replied, "Trust us, it won't." I heard no persuasion, but much propaganda. They offered no reasons for their opinions and did not care to hear the reasons for my concerns.

They may be right. Being right has nothing to do with whether or not their words were propaganda. There was no focus on facts or information, just opinion and emotion. Their manner of speaking aborted discussion.

After that conversation I learned more about the issue from a fact-checking organization. Their arguments challenged the veracity of the information I had. They addressed my concerns point-by-point, and swayed my thinking about the issue. The use of reasoned argument influenced my thinking when the repetition of opinion could not.

Propaganda works when reasoning is not engaged. PowerPhrases use persuasion, and the engagement of reason.

PowerPhrases allow you to tell the simple truth responsibly and be persuasive without using propaganda. You have a point of view based on your knowledge, experience and perceptions. Use PowerPhrases to give others the benefit of your opinion...and to invite them to share theirs. That's what telling the simple truth is about.

Truth by Default

Remember to go to *calculator.com* and ask the Love Calculator about your chances of romantic success. When it asks you if you want it to lie, let your choice for the truth be a symbol of your commitment to truth in life. Set your default mode to truth.

Let truth win by default.

Get *Standards of Responsible Communication* at the SpeakStrong Store.
http://www.speakstrong.com/store/#soc

235

CHAPTER 14

Establish a Code: The Runion Rules of Responsible Communication

"It was a small corporation in a desperate town.
Problems were up. Profits were down.
Morale was rock bottom. Grim was its fate.
They had no code to communicate."

The Legend of Mighty Mouth—*Meryl Runion*
(Available in entirety on enclosed CD)

Turn on a political show and you will see communication chaos at its worst. People substitute opinion for fact, distort truth, hurl judgments and insults at each other and take things out of context. When a commentator agrees with a guest s/he allows them to speak uninterrupted. When a commentator disagrees, they shout the guest down. Is it ever like this in your boardroom or even your living room?

What we need is a code of communication.

What the show needs is a code for communication. I have created one, but I don't expect any takers on the talk shows: ratings would plummet. I have better luck in boardrooms and living rooms.

Television deliberately intensifies tensions to incite discord so the viewers will stay tuned in. In reality you are better off to use every tool available to reduce tension and increase harmony. **The Runion Rules of Responsible Communication** set guidelines for those difficult conversations to make it safe to talk, and to make discussion possible. Before you have a sensitive conversation, discuss, agree to and post the guidelines. Most of all, follow them. The Rules are listed next, with elaboration later in the chapter. (A copy for posting is available on my website, *www.speakstrong.com*, and in the enclosed CD.)

The Runion Rules of Responsible Communication

We agree to observe the following in our communication:

1. **Stay Positive:**

   We emphasize solutions and what we want. We choose our words to elevate and empower each other. We examine problems and hold ourselves and each other accountable, not to blame, but for the purpose of finding solutions.

2. **Be Civil:**

   We are courteous and respectful with each other. We speak the truth without viciousness or attack.

3. **Use Candor:**

   We are straightforward, direct and open.

4. **Speak Accurately and Honestly:**

   We speak with precision, exactness and adherence to facts. We: A) Are balanced in our use of facts, B) Limit ourselves to reasonable interpretation of facts in all claims, C) Observe contextual correctness, and D) Are informative and substantive.

5. **Listen Accountably:**

   We listen more than we speak. We listen as though we will be tested on understanding their words.

6. **Maintain the Three Perspectives:**

   We maintain awareness of the following three perspectives: ours, theirs, and the one a neutral party would tell.

Before you engage in a sensitive discussion, agree to the Runion Rules of Responsible Communication.

We agree to refrain from using:

1. *Sarcasm*

2. *Labeling*

3. *Blame*

4. *Emotional manipulation*

5. *Absolute language*

6. *Threats*

A detailed explanation of the guidelines is included at the end of the chapter. Before reviewing these details, let's take a closer look at why having a communication code is important.

Runion Rules of Responsible Communication: A Closer Look

When a conversation is challenging or controversial, it is easy to feel threatened and go into a fight-or-flight reaction. Chemicals like adrenaline and cortisol are released into your bloodstream. Your respiratory rate increases. Blood is redirected from your digestive tract and into your muscles and limbs. Your pupils dilate. Your vision sharpens. Your awareness intensifies. Your impulses quicken. You become prepared—physically and psychologically—for fight-or-flight. You scan and search your environment, "looking for the enemy."

When your fight-or-flight system is activated, you tend to perceive everything in your environment as a possible threat to survival. By its very nature, the fight-or-flight system bypasses your rational mind—where better thought-out beliefs exist—and moves you into "attack" mode. Everyone and everything becomes a possible enemy.

When communicating, this is not a reaction you want to

Runion Rules of Responsible Communication keep the fight-or-flight response in check.

activate. The **Runion Rules of Responsible Communication** are designed to provide a rational basis for communication, which makes it easier to stay out of reaction.

Let's examine the details of the code more closely.

The Runion Rules of Responsible Communication in Detail

Stay Positive: The Importance of Creating Safety and Vision

Negativity activates defensiveness and the fight-or-flight response. Positivity creates safety and openness. The positive aspect of PowerPhrases creates safety. When the speaker knows that his or her words will be received with good will, they feel free to be honest. If the speaker is fearful of attack, they are likely to censor their words.

Possibility thinking elevates conversation.

Maintaining a positive vision for the outcome throughout a conversation elevates all involved to their highest possible brain functioning. "Possibility thinking" inspires everyone, and ideas flow from a state of inspiration. This does not mean that problems are ignored. However, they are addressed in the light of possibility, which affects the entire tone and outcome of every conversation.

Be Civil

Civility is essential to create safety in communication and to avoid triggering a fight-or-flight reaction. There are many common language practices that belittle the listener, either intentionally or unintentionally. Civility does not mean denying or avoiding difficult realities. It does mean to be respectful, even if at the moment you do not believe the other person deserves respect. To be civil, avoid:

1. **Sarcasm** which makes the person it is directed to the target of ridicule. ("Did you do this all by yourself?")

2. **Labeling and name calling** that stereotypes others and puts them into a limited box. ("You're not a team player.")

3. **Blame** which condemns. The distinction between blame and accountability is difficult to discern. Accountability seeks to understand. Blame attacks. People must be held accountable. Blame is not necessary and is often unproductive. ("This is your fault" vs. "I see some things you could have done to avoid this. Let's look at what they are so this won't happen again.")

4. **Emotional manipulation**, which attempts to place emotional pressure on others. This includes attempts to make someone feel guilty, shaming someone into compliance, deliberately triggering their anger or manipulating their fears. ("If you respected me you would have…" "After all I've done for you…") Any type of emotional manipulation is improper and irresponsible.

5. **Absolute language** that over-simplifies the truth and limits understanding to simplistic, black and white concepts. ("You are with us or you are against us.") "Always" and "never" are examples of black and white language we want to avoid. ("You're always sarcastic.")

6. **Threats** that use coercion to intimidate. They are an attempt to force someone into doing what we want. There is a subtle but important distinction between threatening someone and informing them of the consequence of their action. Threats are intended to limit choice to the path we want them to take. Informing of consequences is intended to inform someone of the choice you

Civility creates safety in conversation.

241

will make based on what they do. For example, "If you value your job, you'll do as you're told" is a threat. "This work is part of your job description and needs to be done. If you are not willing to do it, I'll have to replace you with someone who will" informs of consequences.

Use Candor

One benefit of being straightforward, direct and open is that it creates trust and confidence. Candor dispels the need to deduce meanings, probe for hidden implications, or risk being blindsided. Candor can be uncomfortable in the moment, but combined with civility it ultimately builds relationships. Part of PowerPhrases is to say what you mean and tell the truth about what you think, feel and want.

Candor creates trust.

When a long-lost friend did not receive an answer to an email she had sent me, she correctly surmised that I hadn't received it. She knew if I was angry, I would have told her. She was correct. My previous candor created safety for her. Another friend told me, "Whenever I talk to you I always know you're going to tell me the truth. I depend on that." It is not always easy in the short run to use candor, but in the long run it creates safety.

Speak Accurately and Honesty

Distortion is a violation of the Runion Rules, even if the words spoken are literally true. There are many ways to distort the truth. Statistics can be manipulated, partial truths can mislead and facts can be exaggerated. Sometimes these efforts are deliberate. Other times the speaker maintains the illusion of being truthful.

Responsible communication rejects all forms of deception. Accuracy is essential for effective communication. All parties need to be certain they can trust the veracity of what they hear. Speak with precision, exactness and adherence to facts, including:

1. A balanced use of facts.

Choose facts that are representative of the whole, and avoid the implication that the exception is the rule. For example, if I have thirteen complaints about a procedure and one person who likes it, it would be a distortion for me to speak of the one person who likes it and fail to mention the thirteen complaints. I may be speaking truthfully, but I am distorting the truth.

2. Limit yourselves to reasonable interpretation of facts in all claims.

Only interpret facts in a way any reasonable person might. For example, to say that someone who questioned the efficacy procedure is disloyal is not a reasonable interpretation of the facts.

3. Observe contextual correctness.

Information used out of context is inappropriate and violates trust. If you look for evidence to support any theory, you are likely to be able to find something, especially when used out of context. Accuracy and honesty require that quotes and examples are used to convey the same message they would when provided in context. For example, imagine I say, "I know my boss makes mistakes…we all do…yet I am constantly stunned by his knowledge of the industry and his skill as a manager." Someone who quotes me as saying my boss makes mistakes is being technically truthful, yet inaccurate in the out of context use of quotes.

Responsible communication rejects all forms of deception.

4. Being informative and substantive.

While emotional appeals can be effective, and emotional displays can get results, ultimately it is more productive to be "insightful," than "inciteful." Communicate to educate and add to the understanding of the listener. Make certain all claims have a solid basis of information that is researched and substantiated. For example, if your company is being bought out, there will probably be talk about the job losses that will ensue. This can incite fear in employees. However, the responsible communicator will investigate the history of the acquiring company's former acquisitions and the stated plans before speaking, and will include the basis for their opinions in any discussion.

Listen Accountably

Listening well pays off. It helps you understand the other person's position. It reduces defensiveness. It wins respect. It facilitates problem solving. When you listen, listen as though you were going to be tested on what they say. Listen for the three crucial points: what do they think, what do they feel, and what do they want. Clarify your understanding of these points by saying:

Listen for what they think, feel and want.

- **Let me be sure my understanding is correct. My understanding is that you think..., feel..., and want.... Is my understanding correct?**

This ensures that your assumptions about what they are saying are accurate.

Maintain the Three Perspectives

There are three perspectives to every conversation — yours, mine, and the one a neutral party would tell. It is much easier to view the three perspectives when you are not personally involved, but as soon as there is personal involvement, the blinders go on. Although difficult, it IS possible to be aware of the three perspectives when you are personally involved. Have all parties ask:

- **What do I think, feel, and want?**

- **What do they think, feel and want?**

- **How would a neutral party describe this conversation/situation?**

This technique helps you to stay aware of all three perspectives at all times.

Use the Runion Rules of Responsible Communication or Create Your Own to Elevate Your Conversations

The guidelines provided in this chapter are shown to facilitate and elevate conversations. However, the best guidelines are the ones everyone involved agrees to. Take the Runion Rules as they are, or adapt them to your own preferences. However you go about it, have a code to communicate to transform the way people talk to each other.

> *The best communication guidelines are ones that everyone agrees to. Create your own.*

Beyond Blame: The Dos and Don'ts of Responsibility
http://www.speakstrong.com/articles/speak-strong/beyondblame.html

READ MERYL'S BLOG

Meryl answers perplexing communication questions on her blog.
http://www.speakstrong.com/newsletter/

CHAPTER 15

Meryl Answers the Most Challenging Communication Questions

I love the emails I receive from subscribers who ask how to handle their vexing and perplexing communication challenges. Below are several questions and answers that have been posted in my newsletter. Read on and tell me how I do!

How to Correct the Boss

Meryl:

I have an imposing boss. One time at an important meeting with our technical people, I tried to clear up a paradigm concerning the way a certain piece of equipment works. He said something incorrect about the same piece of equipment in front of this group of people. Putting him on the spot would be counter-productive so how can I right the wrong? I have to get the message out without making him look bad.

Ask people how they want to receive feedback.

MERYL REPLIES:

Have a private discussion with your boss about your issues. What you say depends on how much you are willing to risk. Try these words:

- When my colleagues make mistakes we tell each other immediately, even in meetings. I don't believe that's what you want. Can you tell me how you would like for me to handle it when you say something in a group that isn't completely accurate? This wording is non-confrontational yet direct.

Speaking Truth to Power

I attended one of your workshops in Memphis and found it very informative. I am a student working in an externship at a local place of business. The CEO is a friend. Some of the issues they are dealing with could be easily and correctly addressed with some time spent with you and your books. Communication is a real problem. Because of this poor communication and the individuals' lack of trust in each other, they are unable to do a good job together. Everything is someone else's fault. I will be writing a report to my instructors to finalize my portfolio of this externship in about a month. The CEO may also expect some kind of a report. Given he is a friend and was instrumental in my obtaining this valuable experience, I need to know how to write this report. I need to know how to say what needs to be said, to mean what I say, without seeming naive and judgmental. (I wouldn't be mean when I said it!)

I appreciate any help you can give me.

MERYL REPLIES:

First, ask your friend:

• How honest do you want me to be?

Write your report in the same tone you are writing me. Document specific uses and misuses of words and the consequences you observe. Recommend a code of communication such as **The Runion Rules of Communication**.

Uncomfortable Silence

Meryl, I lost my husband to a heart attack last month. My friends have been a wonderful support to me, but

When you have a tough message, solicit an invitation for honesty before you dive in to the message.

some seem to not know what to say. What do you recommend?

MERYL REPLIES:

Initiate the conversation from your side. Say,

• **It is hard to know what to say at a time like this. I want you to know that I appreciate your friendship, and you don't need to worry about saying the right or wrong thing. Your friendship is enough.**

Saying something right off will alleviate their concerns. If you are genuine, it will encourage them to be genuine with you. Best of luck in this very tough time.

Treated Like a Child

Hi Meryl:

I have a question for you. How do I gain the trust and/or confidence of my boss when I offer creative solutions or ideas to situations that arise? When I have a problem or situation I usually approach him with a couple of different ways we can deal with it. However, I feel as though the ideas I express are not taken seriously. I have started "telling" him what needs to be done, but because of his personality he "pats me on the head and sends me off"—appeasing me as though I am a five-year old. I have been with the company as his assistant for nearly two years. HELP!

MERYL REPLIES:

First, make certain that you are not coming across passively.

Do you discount your words before you speak them with comments like "This is just my idea" or "This may not be right but...?"

Do you use a passive tone of voice?

Are you specific in your recommendations?

If you are genuine it encourages others to be genuine with you.

If you are certain you are communicating assertively, it's time to talk to him about the issue. I see two options.

1. Address the issue in a separate meeting.

2. Address the issue when it happens again.

Some things you might say are:

- I appreciate specific feedback on my suggestions. That is how I will learn.

- When I bring ideas to you I often feel discounted by your response. Are my ideas bad? I want to feel my opinions are valued.

- When you pat me on my head I feel patronized. I do not believe you would respond to a man's recommendations by patting him on the head, and it is inappropriate with me.

- Is there something about the way I present my ideas that diminishes their credibility, or is it the ideas themselves that cause you to not take my ideas seriously?

We teach others how to treat us.

Good luck! Remember, you teach others how to treat you. It is time for you to change the dynamic. If you cannot, find somewhere else where you will be respected. If you stay in that environment too long, your initiative will be driven out of you. Don't let that happen!

Stay Calm While Speaking Strong

Dear Meryl,

I attended your seminar recently in MN. I have been putting into play much of what I learned. I do have one question.

How do I say what I mean, mean what I say without being mean when I say it and without getting emotional? I get teary-eyed just by the mention of conflict or a problem. Any suggestions?

Thanks.

MERYL REPLIES:

I have five quick fixes:

- In the web between your thumb and forefinger there is an acupressure point. Press it. That stops tears.

- Pretend you are asking someone to pass the butter. Use the same tone of voice you would use to do that.

- Practice with someone you trust before you speak.

- Use left-brain words such as, "point number one" etc.

- Breathe slowly and deeply.

The long-term remedy:

Long term, you need to connect with what is going on underneath that causes you to be emotional. Journal all your feelings around issues and standing up for yourself. Many of us have a backlog of emotions that come out in full force when they are triggered. For example, until I finished grieving the death of my husband, I cried about trivial matters like dead bugs and long-distance commercials. Once I did the work of diving into the pain I preferred to avoid, my responses became more appropriate to the situation.

If you have a backlog of emotions, it will be a challenge to stay calm while speaking strong until you have healed them.

This is a process that can take an enormous amount of time, but it is well worth the effort to be emotionally clear, cleansed and current.

No More Loans

Meryl,

I work with a woman who does not manage money well. She has asked me twice to loan her money and twice I said yes. I do not intend to bail her out again, but my questions are: (1) How do I say "No" without making her feel uncomfortable for asking me for money? (2) At the same time, how do I deal with my guilt for saying "No"?

Thank you.

MERYL REPLIES:

I suspect that saying "No" will make you uncomfortable no matter how you say it. Say no anyway. Use words like:

- **(Name), I made an exception to my policy of not lending money because you were in a tough spot. I'm not comfortable lending any more money. If there is some other way I can help you, let me know.**

However awkward saying it feels, it can't feel any worse than saying," Yes" when you mean "No."

If you need to say no, do not let discomfort stop you.

Be Straightforward

I have a 24-year-old single daughter. She lives with three other young, single women who are about the same age. They all regularly attend the same church and social events. My daughter has related to me numerous times, that every time she enters into a conversation with any of the young men attending church or social events, one particular roommate enters the conversation and proceeds to dominate the conversation until my daughter excuses herself. My daughter then begins speaking with someone else only to have the same scenario happen again and again. My daughter feels so bombarded by this behavior that she is seriously thinking of changing residences in the hopes that this behavior will stop.

I would really appreciate any help you can provide with this situation. What can my daughter say to her roommate to stop this annoying and rude behavior?

Thank you.

MERYL REPLIES:

It is not unusual, but it is unfortunate, that people consider quitting jobs, changing vendors and moving out before they give serious thought to speaking the truth about how they are affected by someone's inconsiderate behavior. Has your daughter said anything to her roommate about the issue? She needs to let her roommate know what she feels and wants. A gentle way to begin can be,

- Roommate, I'd like to make a deal that when one of us is talking to a guy, that the other one allow them to continue uninterrupted. Sometimes I want a guy's full attention, and I bet you feel the same way.

If that doesn't work, she'll need to be more straightforward.

- Roommate, I have noticed that when I start talking to a guy, you often join in. When that happens I find it difficult to say what I have to say because I feel that you have stepped in and taken over the conversation. I feel upstaged. How about we circulate separately at events and then tell each other all about it afterward? Will you do that for me?

I suspect the roommate is not at all aware of a problem and simply needs to be told. If she has a certain pattern of behavior, she may need to be told several times.

It is all too common for people to make drastic changes to avoid people rather than telling them when there is a problem.

Fashion Trend Necessity

I have a health problem that elicits unsolicited comments on a regular basis and I could use some ideas on how to respond.

Due to knee surgery which left me with nerve damage in one of my knees, I "feel" pain when anything touches my knee (like skirts or slacks). Consequently, I wear shorts year round. I live in Colorado, and in the winter I wear wool shorts with knee socks. I dress as nicely as I can, given these limitations. My coworkers and employer have no problem with this. Even clients rarely say anything.

My problem is that complete strangers feel very comfortable making critical, sometimes rude, comments. What can I say that is short and will make me feel better without being rude?

Thanks for your weekly reminder to SpeakStrong!

MERYL REPLIES:

Say,

- **I am attempting to start a trend but it's taking longer to catch on than I hoped.**

Or speak the simple truth,

- **It's most comfortable for me because I have sensitive knees.**

When someone offends you, tell the simple truth.

Managing the Micro-Manager

We would like to get some advice on how to deal with a boss who micro-manages everything. Our team of highly capable people is consistently made to feel inadequate and unable to do their job due to our boss' style of leadership. She is always on our "backs" wanting to know every small detail with regard to all aspects of our jobs, giving orders on the "best way" to complete projects and often completely railroading the simplest tasks. We have recently lost one experienced and very valued member of the team who has just resigned because of her management style, and we would like to prevent this from happening again. We have a very committed team which works well together. The micro-manager is the only thing that presents a problem for this team.

We look forward to any suggestions you have on how to deal with this.

MERYL REPLIES:

Your approach will depend on if you can speak for the group or as a group, and how much you are willing to risk. Here is a good approach.

- Boss, I think in the past you may have worked with a staff that needed a lot of supervision. We are blessed here with highly capable people, and the high level of management that may be necessary in less motivated teams is counterproductive here. We value your input and want you to feel adequately "in the loop," and yet we work best when we are allowed to work more independently. Can you think of a way we can find that balance?

I hope your departed coworker made it clear why he left. If he did, the manager may be aware there is a problem and more open to solutions.

Whatever vexing and perplexing situation you face, you will find the best words in the last place you are likely to look…your own heart and mind. Keep your words short, brief and focused, and you may be surprised by what you learn.

Send your
PowerPhrases
questions to
info@SpeakStrong.
com.

Send Meryl your success story and get a SpeakStrong Award.
Send it to: story@speakstrong.com

Chapter 16

PowerPhrases® in Action: Success Stories from A PowerPhrase a Week Subscribers

If PowerPhrases sounds theoretical to you, this chapter will assure you they are not. I receive letters from my newsletter subscribers every week telling me of how PowerPhrases work for them. I include some here to illustrate the real-world effectiveness of PowerPhrases.

Many of the stories talk about how useful the phrase "Say what you mean, mean what you say and don't be mean when you say it" is. Two examples of this follow.

A Case for Asking

I attended both of your sessions at the CSA Conference in April. Thanks for the message "Say what you mean, mean what you say and don't be mean when you say it." I used your system there at the Conference that same day. I approached a couple of health service providers there in the exhibit hall and asked them if they would donate their services to our operations and maintenance employees at our recognition in-service in July. I practiced exactly what you recommended; I made it clear up front that we did not have any money for their service, and can you believe they have agreed to come!

Just ask.

It Was a Win-Win Performance Review

I attended one of your seminars in Georgia and was deeply impacted by your suggestions on how to SpeakStrong. Upon returning to my job, I found that I was able to use the information you shared with us.

One of the employees on my staff complained consistently. It was up to me to address this in a performance review.

I reviewed my notes on your seminar. The words, "Say what you mean and mean what you say without being mean," gave me the foundation I needed. I thought about what I wanted to accomplish. My goal was to make this person realize how important they were to the team and that they had much to offer if they just shared with the rest of the team.

The Power of PowerPhrases might surprise you.

Our meeting went well and we gained something I didn't expect...mutual respect. Furthermore, we both listened to each other and we have taken some amazing steps in improving our department's objectives due to the contribution this person has made since our talk. Your seminar helped me to focus on a realistic, nonthreatening goal and we were able to come out with a win-win situation.

Pippi Power

When people share success stories, I give them a charming stuffed giraffe that I call Pippi, after Pippi Longstocking. The "Pippi Award" is very popular and represents elevating the level of conversation. (I also use a stuffed lizard, "Izzie," to represent the reptilian brain, and low level conversations. See the introduction for more details.) Pippi is very popular in some workplaces. The next story tells how Pippi has become an icon for one organization.

Meryl,

You gave me a Pippi at a seminar for sharing a success story. Here is another. Pippi came to work with me after attending your seminar. At an employee meeting, I explained to the staff about using your Pippi brain instead of Izzie as well as developing the Pippi "way of life." Now Pippi is an icon at my office. When conflict arises, Pippi comes with me to the "resolution meeting" between the conflicting parties. Whoever holds Pippi is the person allowed to speak. When they are through, Pippi is placed in the center of the table. Then the next person who holds Pippi can reply or speak their mind. The rules are: no fighting over Pippi and everyone must keep a civil tongue. This has worked very well. It keeps arguing to a minimum, and only one person is speaking at a time. Also, if a person happens to pause to think of what they want to say-no one can "butt in" while they are thinking. Pippi helps us come to a resolution in a timely, respectful manner. Thank you.

Get Back to a Positive Dynamic

This next letter illustrates the importance of staying focused on the desired outcome of conversation. It can be difficult to reach out to someone whom we are at odds with. This subscriber succeeded and was able to keep her "Izzie" in check in order to give her coworker what she needed to create resolution.

Meryl,

I recently experienced a success I would like to share with you, particularly since you helped me to achieve it. Besides having both your books, I print your newsletters and put them in a binder. I highlight the items that I think I need. In Issue 96 I found the approach that bailed me out of an uncomfortable situation. It was "Get Back to a Positive Dynamic." A

There is power in having a symbol for your communication commitment.

coworker (in our corporate office) and I have been getting on each others' nerves, and the result has been some fairly snippy emails. I could see the situation was getting worse, not better, and it was not helped when I inadvertently did do something inappropriate. When I realized it, I emailed her back acknowledging my mistake and inviting her to call me back when she had time to let me know what I could do to improve our relationship, with the hope that we could get to a better level of understanding and cooperation. She called me back immediately and pretty frankly told me how she felt. It was very reminiscent of an exercise you had us do in your communication seminar. I acknowledged my mistake and, without rationalizing, explained what my motive had been. Our relationship has advanced to a whole new level. So…. thank you

Sometimes you need to let someone speak their peace.

The referenced exercise involves one partner inventing an issue with their partner and complaining about it. The listener listens to understand what the complainer thinks, feels and wants, and repeats their understanding of it back to the one speaking. Even though people know the issue is imaginary, they still experience their "Izzie's" tensing up. I was happy to hear that the reader was able to refer back to the experience and stay detached in action.

She Took Care of It Her Way

One of the things PowerPhrases emphasize is creativity in your response. You may think your choices are to either acquiesce or confront. In truth you always have far more options. This person handled a situation creatively without bottling or blowing.

Meryl,

At work, I've been asked on many occasions to redo another assistant's work because of poor printing qual-

ity, typographical errors or incorrect information. Several times I've inquired as to why the assistant is not held accountable, but have never received an answer. Rather I'm just asked to please correct her work. A few weeks ago, I was once again asked to "take care of it" and my response was a positive and cheerful, "I'll be glad to take care of it." I promptly returned to my desk and sent a message to the assistant notifying her that, "at Mr. Brown's request, please reprint the brochure with the following changes," and I listed the corrections that needed to take place. Needless to say, the assistant learned to correct her own work; I was able to get back to my workload. I gained a new respect from my boss.

Thank you, Meryl, for your newsletter. I have gained quite a bit of confidence in handling some very challenging situations.

A Supervisor Finds a Better Language

People often tell me PowerPhrases sound like simple common sense. They are right. The simplicity of PowerPhrases is what makes them so powerful. We often don't use common sense in our communication. Instead we let Izzie, our reptilian brain, run the show. What I love about this next letter is what I call the BFO this subscriber had. They had a blinding flash of the obvious. Read on.

Meryl

I used to yell at employees. I established a respond vs. react policy where we decided as an office to communicate without yelling.

One time an employee came in yelling, telling me what to do. I was tempted to tell her a thing or two, but instead I said,

PowerPhrases consider options.

261

> • When you talk to me like this, it is hard for me not to get defensive and yell back. Let's meet again and discuss this in the morning.

I heard that she told everyone she was shocked that I didn't yell. The next morning she came in and apologized for how she had spoken. Our relationship became one of mutual respect, and I found that maintaining control helped me as a supervisor.

Sometimes all we have to do is discover a different way of communication, and it becomes the obvious choice for future communication.

That Liberated Feeling

Many times when we speak about what a group is ignoring, we become the group hero.

Every group has its own culture, and every group has its own verbal prohibitions. It can be risky to bring up an issue that is considered off-limits to the group, but what we are afraid to say is exactly what needs to be said. Many times, by speaking the unspeakable, we become the group hero, and keep tensions from intensifying. It has been wisely said that every group is as healthy as its secrets.

Meryl

I belong to a small group of friends which meets twice a month. At our last two meetings it was apparent that there was something really bothering a particular friend in the group. She had been very quiet during our discussions. Because she is a friend of mine it had been weighing on me, so I decided to confront her. I discovered in talking with her that she had a problem with the way arrangements had been made for the meetings. I urged her to speak with the individual with whom she had the problem. Together we came up with a solution for the future for scheduling meetings. I also urged her to come to me with an issue in the future when she has one. This direct approach is something new for me. I am generally very non-confrontational. How liberating this was to get this out in the open and past us. While amends still need to be made between my two other friends I am hoping that in my taking this step, she will do the same. Thank you for giving me the confidence to face these challenges head on.

Say "No" to Negativity

Many people wait until issues reach a ridiculous level before addressing them. Then, once they address the issue, they have a revelation about how simple it can be to tell the truth. This next reader found setting boundaries worked well for her.

Meryl

I had a coworker who consistently confided her negativity to me. I finally had enough of it when I realized that I was taking it all in and becoming negative myself.

I called her aside and told her,

- **I care about you, but when you complain it makes me get negative myself. I am happy to talk with you, but don't want to hear anything negative anymore.**

It worked, and I don't cringe anymore when I see her walk in.

That last sentence is key to me. "I no longer cringe when I see her walk in." It is usually better for everyone when we tell the truth.

An "Inconvenient Disability"

If you have a reoccurring situation, it is particularly important to have your PowerPhrases ready. I'm sure every flight attendant in the country has a response for the question, "What's for dinner?" Some of my

Even if someone does not want to hear the truth, they usually are better off when they do.

263

subscribers have physical challenges that present regular communication challenges. Here is an example of one such situation.

Meryl,

In December 1994 I was in a car accident and fractured my skull. I lost almost all of my hearing. I wear a hearing aid which enables me to hear when people speak clearly.

At work a customer mumbled at me. I asked him several times to repeat himself and still did not understand what he was saying. Upon my fourth request for him to repeat himself, he said,

— *What's your problem? Are you deaf?*

I responded in a very calm tone of voice,

• **Well, yes, I am deaf. I see it is as inconvenient for you right now as it is for me.**

He slowed down and spoke clearly.

Educate rather than retaliate.

It is easy to resent the kind of unconsciousness required to make a comment like that. However, it is far better to use a PowerPhrase to educate rather than retaliate.

Hire the Attitude

Many people do not realize the power they have in interviews. If you excel in the interview, you are likely to excel in the job. If you take the initiative in the interview, you are likely to take the initiative in the job. If you are confident in the interview, you are likely to be confident in the job. This is demonstrated in the following letter.

Meryl,

I applied for a position twice to no avail. A few years later the position became vacant again.

I applied and the interview process went through three levels. I made it to the third level—to interview with a manager. During my interview, I confessed up front that I lacked the computer skills they required. Additionally, I emphasized my good skills: I was bright, highly motivated and a very quick study. I knew that the interview had gone well. As I rose to depart and shake the manager's hand, I said,

- Hire the attitude and teach the skills; I won't let you down.

Needless to say, I was hired. I love my job, my duties have been expanded and I am very happy.

I Can Hear You.

Often people think the rules are different for communication with the boss. The only difference is the stakes are higher. It is obvious that you need to choose your words with care when speaking to the boss. The truth is, it is important to choose words with care with everyone.

Sincerely letting an interviewer know how much you want a job can pay off.

The following is an example of someone who set a boundary with her boss while reinforcing his role. She did an excellent job, and it worked beautifully.

Meryl,

When I worked for a pizza parlor I had a supervisor who thought I had not been doing my job and came at me yelling at the top of his lungs. I put up my hand and said,

- Sam, I know you are my boss and I respect your authority. You don't need to yell at me to get results.

He never yelled at me again.

This was brilliant. She communicated respect while setting boundaries. Many people would have held on to resentment and quit rather than speak up about inappropriate behavior.

Ask and Ye Shall Receive

This next story demonstrates the importance of being a player in your own performance reviews, as well as the importance of speaking up, even with your boss.

About a month ago I went through a review process with my employer. The objective was to discuss my past year and discuss what my goals were for the next year. During that process, my employer made it quite clear that he wanted me to take more of a "leadership" role and help lead the company in the areas of my knowledge and expertise. A portion of my job is financial and 1 week before my review I completed a 4 month process of redeveloping our financial model and constructing our budget for 2003. When I presented the completed budget to him, I expected him to be pleased that I had resolved the discrepancies and completed it on time.

He quickly pointed out some small notations that I hadn't modified for the forthcoming year and picked my report apart explaining to me that leadership meant presenting an "error free" report. I told him I realized my mistakes and took responsibility for them. I would be sure that I didn't make the mistakes again. I also mentioned that he knew that I had worked very hard on that project and that I was expecting him to be pleased with me. He was taken aback. He said (very sincerely), "Y'know, you're absolutely right. I am sorry. You did work long and hard on that project and did complete it on time. Thank you." I sat there graciously receiving his compliment but inside I was stunned that what I had said had the impact it did.

Many of us would be silent at the review, and then tell

You can make a difference in a performance review.

five friends about the unfairness of it all. This subscriber took a much better option.

Tardiness Cuts into My Time

I always recommend addressing issues at the peer level before complaining to management. I also recommend giving people the benefit of the doubt before making accusations. A PowerPhrase is as strong as it needs to be and not stronger. This next letter shows how a difficult situation was resolved very simply.

Meryl,

One of my co-workers is consistently late to work. While it is usually only 5 or 10 minutes, this means I can't take my lunch until she arrives—which also means I have to cut my lunch short. If this happened only a few times I wouldn't have a problem with it, but it happens at least twice a week. I told her,

- You may not realize this, but I cannot take my lunch until you have arrived. This means that if you're 10 minutes late, that's 10 minutes off of my 40 minute break—which creates a problem for me. How do you suggest we handle this?

That is all it took. I didn't even need to involve management. She came in on time the next day and has been coming in on time ever since.

Some situations can be resolved very simply by telling what we think, feel and want.

Ask Me First Before Reacting

It is important to recognize when we are in reaction and likely to speak in a way we would regret later. This next letter comes from someone who managed to control an angry response and was glad she did.

Meryl,

Recently a coworker sent me an angry email based on inaccurate information from a third party. I was offended and very tempted to fire back an equally angry response.

Instead, I first gave myself time to calm down and then went to see him personally. I told him:

- I was upset when I received your email and I was tempted to fire an angry email back. I decided not to because I thought I may have misunderstood you. I was disappointed that you took someone else's word for what happened rather than asking me.

He told me he felt regret soon after sending the email but didn't know how to bring the issue up himself. He was relieved that I said something so we could clear the air.

Note the final line. He was glad she said something so they could clear the air. By speaking up, this woman was doing both of them a favor. Many people would welcome the discussion of issues...they just don't know how.

Many people are open to discuss issues, but don't initiate it because they don't know how.

I Invite Your Stories

What situations have you turned around by Speaking Strong? Email them to *success@speakstrong.com*. I will use it in my weekly newsletter and send you a Pippi giraffe as an award.

CHAPTER 17:

Silence Is the Greatest PowerPhrase® of All.

The purpose of words is to create silence."

— *Pundit Ravi Shankar*

Throughout the book I have been an advocate for speaking up, and saying what needs to be said. I have written about the high cost of silence. I have implored you to say what needs to be said.

Now I will make a case for silence.

When you don't have anything to say, choose silence.
When you want to punctuate a point, choose silence.
When you can't be heard over the noise, choose silence.
When everything has been said, choose silence.

Some words create agitation. Some words result in questions. Some words cause confusion. True Power-Phrases result in silence.

Silence is the ultimate PowerPhrase.

True PowerPhrases produce peace. True PowerPhrases resolve questions. True PowerPhrases clear up confusion.

Remember from the introduction:

• **Less is more.**

Powerful communicators know when to speak and when to be quiet. Powerful communicators are not afraid of silence. Silence is the ultimate PowerPhrase.

PowerPhrases® Quick Reference Guide

Contents:

Acknowledging Comments Without Agreeing

(Particularly Useful to Defuse Anger)
- I can see you feel strongly about this.
- I did not know you felt that way.
- I see. Tell me more.
- What else concerns you?
- The point you made about ___ hits home.
- I don't blame you for being upset about...
- I hate it when that happens to me too!
- I get angry too when...
- I appreciate you sharing your experience. What else do I need to know?
- That may be.
- I might feel that way if I was in your shoes.
- That's an interesting perspective.
- I did not realize that you felt that way.
- I had not considered that perspective.

Acknowledgment/Compliments

- I appreciate ___ because...
- When you ___ I felt ___ because...
- Here are the reasons I value you (your)...
- I am grateful because...

Advice/Recommendations/Suggestions

- What I like about what you did is… There are a lot of things I do differently. Would you like to hear my thoughts?

- What struck me most is… What I suggest you do to make it even better next time is…

- Have you considered doing it this way?

- You know your job a lot better than I do, so my questions may be irrelevant. If so please tell me they are and tell me why. Why do you do things that way?

- What would happen if you…?

- I think you are good at what you do, and my job is to make your performance the best it can be. I want to understand your job and to see if there is anything I can recommend that will make your job easier.

Anger—Defusing and Responding to

- I can understand that.

- I can see why you would see it that way.

- You have put a lot of energy into…

- You're right, you…

- You do have a right to…

- Are you open to hearing my ideas about…?

- I can understand why you would be upset about…

- ___ is important to you, and my actions violated that.

- I want to resolve this because…

- I'm sorry this misunderstanding happened because I care about our relationship.

- I value your account and take your concerns to heart.

- I understand you're upset and your anger will not get me to change my policy.
- If I could give you what you are asking for I would without your anger. I can't and your anger will not change that.
- I am frightened by anger.
- I am not frightened by anger.
- I want to focus on the issues but I find the intensity of your words distracting.
- It was not my intention to offend you.
- I'm sorry I wasn't clear.

Anger—Expressing

- I am angry because...
- That makes me angry...
- The reason why my blood feels like it's boiling when that happens is because...
- I am furious about...
- I feel discounted because....
- I'm frustrated because (I have been on the phone for over forty minutes and shuffled from department to department thirteen times and still don't have the person who can help me.)
- I feel unvalued when....
- I am embarrassed and feel violated by...
- If this doesn't change I will...
- I need as much specific information as you can give me because I will discuss this with my attorney to see what my options are.
- In order to be able to continue here I need...

Apologizing Without Groveling

- I'm sorry. I didn't mean to offend you.
- I'm sorry. I truly intended to be helpful.
- I apologize. I did not mean to come across that way.
- What I said (did) was inappropriate because…
- Please forgive me.
- How can I make it up to you?
- You were counting on me and I let you down.
- I value our friendship and it makes me sad to know I did something that weakened it.
- I care about you and what I did doesn't honor that.
- I hate to see you hurting and hate it even more to know I caused it.

Complaining Effectively

- I need your help. I am not happy with the service/product because…
- I understand that your policy entitles me to…
- If this is not resolved I will…
- This is not what I usually experience with this company.
- I know your company places a high value on customer satisfaction.
- What I want is…
- This is a problem. We need to find a solution.
- This is unacceptable and needs to be addressed.
- I need your help to resolve this.
- I am angry about this delay. How do you plan to get back on schedule after this delay?
- I have been here for three months and do not have a workstation. I am frustrated because I lose valuable time reorganizing my papers, supplies and thoughts at each new desk. My request is that when the next person leaves, I get the vacated workstation.

- When you read the paper while I am speaking I feel ignored. I would like your full attention and eye contact when I speak.
- I sent three inquiries without receiving a response. I think I am being ignored. Going forward I need a response within two days.

Compliments—Accepting

- Thank you. That means a lot, especially from you.
- Thank you. It helped that I had such great support from my team.
- Thank you. I feel great about it too.
- Thank you for noticing.

Conflict—Addressing

- There is an issue I'd like to discuss. Can we meet?
- ___ is creating problems.
- The effect is…
- I/we feel…
- What happens is…
- I understand…
- I appreciate…
- I want…
- I need…
- I prefer…
- That may be.
- I see this is a big issue for you.
- I didn't realize that was an issue for you.
- How can we make this work for both of us?
- What can I do to make you want to give me what I want here?
- Let's see if we can find a solution that works for both of us.

- Let's implement what we've decided and review how well it's working.
- I can understand why you would be upset about...
- Accountability is important to you, and by ___ I can see that I was not accountable.
- If this continues I will...
- If this doesn't change I won't...

Criticism or Complaints-Receiving

- I wasn't aware there was a problem. I want to hear your feedback to understand what needs to be changed.
- I understand why you viewed it that way. Next time, I will handle it by doing...
- I want to do whatever I can to strengthen our working relationship. I consider us a team.
- I will use this information to devise a plan to improve my performance.
- What else would you like to see me do differently?
- Could you be more specific? What do you mean by...?
- Do I understand you correctly that...?
- What needs to be done at this point?
- Thanks for giving me your feedback. It is helpful for me to know how you view it.
- Tell me more.
- What else do you want to tell me?
- I will consider everything you told me and see how I can apply it.

Delegation—Encouraging Buy-In

- I am aware of how busy you are. However, I have a request...
- I would never ask you to do something I would not do myself...
- There is an opportunity here for you to...
- I'm asking you because I know I can trust you...
- I have a project I can only trust my very best rep (manager, engineer etc.) with.
- I need your help.
- I have a project I think you will enjoy that is outside your usual area.

Delegation—Giving Directions and Ensuring Clarity

- I need _____ by _____ because_____.
- Here is what needs to happen...
- I have written out instructions. Let's go over them together.
- The deadline is ___.
- The quality specifications are ___.
- The budget is ___.
- Of these three, the priority in this project is ___.
- An example of what it will look like is...
- It is crucial that this is done exactly as I show you because...
- I have found that unless we walk through the process, there will be errors. Therefore, please bear with me as we walk through the process together.
- Let me make sure my instructions were clear. What is your understanding of how to do this?
- What questions have I not answered for you?
- What else can I tell you to be sure it's completely clear?

Delegation—Offering a Benefit

- What this means to you is...
- This will help you by...
- If you do this for me I will...
- I'll make sure my boss knows how you made a difference when I really needed you.
- This will be good, not only for me and the team, but for you because...

Disagreeing Gracefully

- You're right, and I have a different opinion.
- I see it differently.
- That's one perspective. I have a different one.
- That may be. What makes sense to me is...
- You may be right. Let's look at the facts and see.
- That's an interesting perspective. What if...
- It looks like we are in agreement about a couple of things here...Where we are still at odds is...
- To really understand your point, I need specific examples.
- What I hear you saying is... Is my understanding correct?
- You just said that ... (I lied, I am stupid, etc...) Will you explain what you mean by that?
- Please continue.
- Your intentions are not clear to me. Can you help me out here?
- I have listened carefully to understand your position. Will you give me five minutes of uninterrupted time to explain mine?
- You make valid points that make a lot of sense from where you stand. Please hear me out as I describe how it looks to me.
- Are you ready to hear how I see it?

- I see it differently.
- You're right. My thoughts are…
- Help me to understand how you see it that way.
- Can you clarify that?

Listening to Encourage Openness

- I want to hear what you have to say.
- I didn't know you felt that way. Tell me more.
- I see why that would be an issue for you.
- I can imagine how that might have felt.
- Tell me more.
- What else can you tell me about that?
- That's an interesting point.
- What did you like about that?
- Help me to understand.
- I'm a bit confused about…
- What were you referring to when you said…?
- I didn't catch something you said a minute ago.
- Let me make sure I understand what you are saying. I believe you are saying…
- So when ___ happened you felt___?
- What you need from me is… Am I right?
- I appreciate you being so open with me.
- You can talk to me.
- I want to hear what you have to say.

Negotiation

- Let's discuss the situation and come up with a solution we both are happy with. I do not want either of us to agree to anything that does not satisfy both our needs.

- What goals do you have for today?

- How would you like to see this discussion turn out?

- Let's talk specifics and see if there is a way we can make this work.

- In my view, a fair solution would be...

- Do you have any concerns with this proposal?

- Based on my research your offer seems out of range.

- I cannot come close to that because of the cost involved.

- How did you arrive at that figure?

- If you were in my seat would you consider that a reasonable offer?

- While I agree on the whole, I have trouble agreeing with the point about...

Put-Downs—Responses To

- I thought I heard a dig. Did I?

- That remark hurts because I care about your opinion and it sounds like you are trying to discourage me. If you have an issue, let's discuss it directly.

- I worked very hard to (make this party a success). If I have not met your expectations, tell me what's wrong, but don't take pot shots.

- I think that remark was hurtful and uncalled for.

- I feel disappointed and affronted.

- I want to be treated with respect.

- I think there must be something else bothering you for you to make a remark like that.

- I feel offended.

- I want to discuss anything that may be creating tension between us.

- That remark sounded like a dig.
- I am insulted.
- I expect to be treated with respect.
- That's your opinion. I see it differently.
- I am interested in your opinions, but not in your insults.
- Ouch! How inappropriate...

Questions—Asking

- Have you ever had the experience...?
- What do you do when...?
- Wouldn't you like to...?
- Can you imagine...?
- How do you do this process?
- What is your understanding of...?
- What do you know about...?
- What I heard you say was...
- I'm interested in learning about... What can you tell me?
- Let me ask you this ...
- Help me understand...?
- Could you help me with...?
- Could you expand on that for me...?
- Are you committing to...?
- Are you saying that...?

Questions—Responding to Challenging

- Why do you ask that?
- Are you asking me if...?

- What specifically do you want to know about...?
- How would YOU respond to that question?
- That question is phrased in a way that sets up the answer. I think a fairer question is...

Refusal/Saying No— ACT Formula: Acknowledge/Circumstance/Transform

A) *Acknowledge*

- Thanks for asking...
- I appreciate you thinking of me...
- That sounds like a worthwhile project...
- I see you need help here...
- I wish I could...

B) *Circumstance*

- I'm not comfortable...
- I would feel awkward...
- I have other priorities...
- I'm already committed...
- It doesn't work for me...
- I won't be able to...
- I don't want to...

C) *Transform/Tag*

- Thanks again for asking.
- Maybe next time.
- I hope you get the help you need.
- Let's do something else sometime.

Refusal/Saying NO—ACT Formula Applied

- I understand this is important. My situation is... Perhaps next time.
- I appreciate you thinking of me. I have other plans. I'm sure you'll find the person you need.
- I wish I could help out here. I'm not well-suited to do what you want. Here's an option...
- I see you need help. After looking at my calendar I see I can't give you the help you need. Have you considered asking ___?
- I'm honored that you thought of me. After realizing the scope of the request, I choose to pass. I wish you success.
- Thanks for asking. Not this time.
- Sounds interesting. I have other commitments
- My policy is...
- I know this is important. I'm working on... What can I put aside to make time to complete this?

Small Talk/Conversational PowerPhrases

- What led you to do the kind of work you are doing?
- What do you enjoy most about the work you do?
- What did you like best about your vacation?
- What do you like about where you live?
- What advice would you give someone just starting in your business?
- Tell me about...
- The turnout is huge! I came for the talk on eWidgets. What brings you here?
- What got you interested in that?
- I want to get to know you better because...

- I am here because I am looking for information about…
- I'm looking for a good movie. Got any recommendations?
- What do you do to relax?
- What do you enjoy about your job?
- I'm in the publishing industry. How about you?
- Tell me about your family.
- That's a lovely necklace. What is the story behind it?
- What would you recommend to someone who has never been here before?
- What did you do before you worked here?

Find your communication style online at:
http://www.speakstrong.com/inventory/

Communication Tendencies Based on Personality

Based on your personality and communication style, some aspects of using PowerPhrases will be easier for you than others. PowerPhrases are short, specific, focused expressions that say what you mean (think, feel and want), and mean what you say without being mean when you say it.

Some personality styles are naturally brief. Others are naturally specific. Some personality styles only open their mouths with a goal clearly in mind. Some find it easier to say what they mean and mean what they say than others. Some naturally consider the effect of their words while others don't. What is easy for some is difficult for others.

Take the personality test to determine your style, and then review the PowerPhrases strengths, weaknesses and recommendations to determine where you need to focus to enhance your PowerPhrase potential.

Communication Evaluation

The enclosed CD Rom has a link for the test online which will do the scoring for you.

1. **P** When I'm in line at the store, I might initiate a chat with the person ahead of me.

   T When I'm in line at the store, I would be unlikely to chat with the person ahead of me unless they initiate it.

2. **T** I like to stay focused on the subject at hand and prefer not to go off on tangents

   P I like to go wherever a conversation leads me.

3. **C** In a buffet line people find themselves waiting for me to finish serving myself.

   S In a buffet line I often find myself waiting for others to finish serving themselves.

4. C If I am at a red light at 3 AM with no one around I wait for it to change to proceed.

    S If I am at a red light at 3 AM with no one around I go on through.

5. T I study the research before deciding what to buy.

    P I consult my friends before deciding what to buy.

6. C Sometimes people finish my sentences for me.

    S Sometimes I finish other people's sentences for them.

7. C I do one thing at a time until it is completed.

    S I work on several things at a time.

8. P I am open about my feelings.

    T I am careful about whom I share my feelings with.

9. T I speak on a need-to-know basis.

    P I enjoy disclosing who I am to develop relationships with people.

10. T When I get excited, everyone around me knows.

    P When I get excited most people can't tell.

11. C I planned the outgoing message on my voicemail before I recorded it.

    S I recorded my outgoing voicemail without rehearsal.

12. P I gladly put aside what I am working on when someone needs help.

    T I ask questions about what is needed and consider what I am doing first before responding when someone needs help.

13. T I have my day clearly planned out early.

    P While I may have an idea of what I want to accomplish, I stay flexible to see how the day unfolds.

14. S I'll let you know right away if you do something that creates problems for me.

    C I will deliberate carefully over whether or not to let you know if you do something that creates problems for me.

15. S I decide within five minutes what I think of a movie.

    C I am waiting until I have had time to reflect to decide what I think of a movie.

16.   S   If I see something I want at a store I get it right away.

      C   When I see something I want at a store I wait and decide if I really want it.

17.   P   If I want to see a movie I'll try to find someone to go with me and won't go if I can't get anyone.

      T   If I want to see a movie I'm happy to go alone.

18.   C   I get my favorite dishes at restaurants.

      S   I like to try new dishes when dining out.

TOTAL NUMBER OF CIRCLED

P _____   T _____   C _____   S _____

Add up your P's, your T's, your C's and S's. Your T's and P's should total 9 and your C's and S's also should total 9.

P's stand for **People-Oriented** and T's stand for **Task-Oriented**, C's stand for a **Careful Pace** and S's stand for a **Swift Pace**.

If you have more P's than T's you are **People-Oriented**. If you have more T's than P's you are a **Task-Oriented**. Record your orientation.

If you have more C's than S's you have a **Careful Pace**. If you have more S's than C's you have a **Swift Pace**. Record your pace.

If you are: **People-Oriented** with a **Careful Pace** you are a *Likeable*

If you are: **People-Oriented** with a **Swift Pace** you are a *Visionary*

If you are: **Task-Oriented** with a **Swift Pace** you are an *Achiever*

If you are: **Task-Oriented** with a **Careful Pace** you are a *Reflective*

Read the section below that applies to you, and discover what your PowerPhrase strengths and areas for development are. We all have some overlap, so review other sections you relate to as well, especially if you were borderline between types.

Likeable: People-Oriented with a Careful Pace

You are social and you take your time in life. As a result, you speak in a very personal manner. It's not about things for you, it's about people. You make your associates your friends and you care about the details in their lives. You measure your success by the relationships you develop.

The table below evaluates the Likeable communication style according to the PowerPhrase principles, and highlights your strengths and areas for development. PowerPhrases are short, specific, focused expressions that say what you mean (think, feel and want), and mean what you say without being mean when you say it.

PowerPhrase Principle	Likeable Strengths	Likeable Areas For Development
Short	You are very good at listening, and saying just enough to reinforce others when they need to be heard.	Learn to be brief. You like to tell the whole story, starting at birth and filling in all the details. You have so much fun in the process of talking that you are unconcerned about making a point. You will talk for talking's sake, and you will talk to make personal connections. This can be maddening for someone who is goal oriented.

PowerPhrase Principle	Likeable Strengths	Likeable Areas For Development
Specific	You are very specific about feelings and no one ever wonders if you care about them or not. Your words cause people to feel heard and understood, sometimes better than they understand themselves. People crawl right into your heart. Your words endear others.	Get specific even if it is uncomfortable to do so. You don't like conflict, and if there is a chance an issue will cause discomfort, you tend to be indirect and whitewash the issue. Therefore things can fester. Sometimes to avoid a reaction you will hint rather than ask for what you want, hoping the other person will guess.
Focused/Targeted	While you do not tend to be goal oriented overall, there is one goal that you pursue naturally. That is harmony.	Get focused on outcome. You can sound indecisive, and sometimes you are! You see all sides of an issue and empathize with the wants and needs of others so much that you can find it difficult to come down on one side and focus on a goal.
Say What You Mean (Think)	When your thoughts are in alignment with others, you let them know.	Get real about what you think, even if your opinions are unpopular. Too often you wait to hear the opinions of others to determine what is safe to say. Your opinions matter.
Say What You Mean (Feel)	When you like and/or appreciate someone, they know! You open your heart and let the love, goodwill and appreciation flow out.	Get objective about your feelings. Sometimes you gush and can seem overly emotional, which can reduce your credibility. You sometimes display emotions rather than disclose them. Your feelings are important, but if you speak FROM your feelings rather than ABOUT them, you set yourself up to be dismissed as too emotional. Sometimes you will be too personal for the comfort of others.

PowerPhrase Principle	Likeable Strengths	Likeable Areas For Development
Say What You Mean (Want)	You are very good at speaking about what other people want. For example, if your child needs an advocate, you can communicate what is needed very well.	Be your own advocate about what you want. You will agree to things you don't want to do rather than risk upsetting someone. That either overwhelms you or causes you to not be able to deliver on promises. Often you are reluctant to ask for what you want, hoping others will guess.
Mean What You Say	You are very sincere in your acknowledgement for others. You are reliable in your commitments except when you over commit.	Back your words up with action. You can over-promise, which causes you to under deliver. People learn that you don't always back up boundaries you set, and some realize they can get you to back down. You think you're being nice, but nice is sometimes a euphemism for "push-over."
Don't Be Mean When You Say It	When it comes to affirming people, you are there! You have a wonderful way of building bridges, creating consensus in teams and getting everyone involved. People feel safe with you because of your extraordinary kindness and compassion.	Your lack of directness can cause you to be passive–aggressive about communicating issues. You sometimes bottle and blow.

Likeable PowerPhrase Prescriptions: Below are phrases that you probably don't use enough…and need to.

Short:

- I have two points I want to make and I need three minutes of your time.
- I'll be brief.
- I'll make a long story short.
- What's the bottom line on this?

Specific:
- When you___ the effect was…
- What I want is ___. Can you do that for me?
- That was inappropriate because…

Targeted:
- I have made a decision in this matter.
- What I want to accomplish is…
- Let's make sure we…

Say What You Mean: Thoughts
- I see it differently.
- This is an issue that needs to be addressed.
- Let me tell you what I think.

Say What You Mean: Feelings
- I feel ___about…
- That upsets me.
- I am frustrated by…

Say What You Mean: Wants
- That doesn't work for me. What would work is…
- What I want is…
- Would you please…?

Mean What You Say:
- I am holding you accountable for what you did.
- I said what I meant and meant what I said.
- I will not yield to pressure.
- You can file a complaint if you want to, however it will not change my decision.

Visionary: People-Oriented with a Swift Pace

You are highly social and like to be on the go. It's about fun and adventure for you. You tend to be the center of attention in any group and that's the way you like it. You look toward the future and are full of ideas of possibilities. You thrive on change and innovation. You appeal to the imagination of your listener. People find your words inspiring and find themselves persuaded by you. You are idealistic and visionary, and you can inspire vision in others and motivate them. You also are very fun!

The table below evaluates the Visionary communication style according to the PowerPhrase principles, and highlights your strengths and areas for development. PowerPhrases are short, specific, focused expressions that say what you mean (think, feel and want), and mean what you say without being mean when you say it.

PowerPhrase Principle	Visionary Strengths	Visionary Areas For Development
Short	You do not overload people with details.	If in doubt, leave it out. Visionaries enjoy talking. You like the spotlight, and you like an audience. Therefore you will talk whether or not you have anything to say. This diminishes the impact of your words.
Specific	You are very good at metaphors and simple ways to describe your point so that others know exactly what you mean.	Just the facts, Ma'am (or Sir). Just the facts. You often play fast and loose with facts. You exaggerate and approximate without realizing how it loses you credibility. Get more precise and exacting in your choice of words.

PowerPhrase Principle	Visionary Strengths	Visionary Areas For Development
Targeted	Your goals are comprehensive and inclusive. You always have your eye on the big picture.	Pick you desired outcome and get targeted. While you are great on inspiration, you can lack follow-through. Your words are often scattered, unfocused and lose sight of the steps required to get results. Your speech can be tangential, which is confusing to those whose speech patterns flow logically.
Say What You Mean (Think, Feel, Want)	You are open and that creates openness in others. Your belief is that truth and openness can solve all problems, and every issue can be resolved if you talk it through. Often you are right, and your optimism and earnestness breaks barriers.	Get discriminating. You sometimes say what you mean to a fault, and can open your mouth and put your foot right in, diminishing your effectiveness. When I tell you to say what you mean. I am not suggesting you say everything you mean. There is a time and place for everything…and Visionaries can overlook this. Visionaries like to share every thought, feeling and desire that pops into their heads. Balance your desire to talk and be open with discretion, and remember goals and the words likely to support your goals.
Mean What You Say	You are sincere.	Get dependable. Your eternal optimism causes you to over commit and fall short of fulfilling promises. Your tendency to exaggerate can build expectations you cannot realize. Pay attention to what you promise, and be more attentive to deliver what you say you will.
Don't Be Mean When You Say It	Your natural appreciation of others causes you to see their best side and communicate that. You look for the good and find it if it's there!	Think it over. Sometimes your haste causes you to be insensitive to the feelings of others. You can open your mouth and say things you would not have said had you given it more thought.

Visionary PowerPhrase Prescriptions: Below are phrases that you probably don't
use enough...and need to.

Short:
- Let's get to the point.
- My point is...
- I'll summarize quickly.

Specific:
- To be specific...
- The practical considerations are...
- I want to represent the possibilities accurately.
- I don't want to mislead you.

Focused/targeted:
- I want to complete this before I move on to something new.
- There are three things to consider here. First...
- The relevant facts are...

Say What You Mean:
- I will stick to the relevant details.
- The key points are...
- That information is confidential.

Mean What You Say:
- I promised this, and I will deliver.
- You can count on my word.

Achiever: Task-Oriented with a Swift Pace

You are very focused and results-oriented. You want what you want and you want it NOW, with little patience for excuses or social nicety. You are Task-Oriented and move at a fast pace. "Just make it happen" is one of your mantras.

The table below evaluates the Achiever communication style according to the PowerPhrase principles, and highlights the strengths and areas for development. PowerPhrases are short, specific, focused expressions that say what you mean (think, feel and want), and mean what you say without being mean when you say it.

PowerPhrase Principle	Achiever Strengths	Achiever Areas For Development
Short	When it comes to being brief, you are there! You make your point quickly and in certain terms. You do not waste any time.	Get connected. You take brevity to the extreme. You can be so brief as to come across as abrupt and abrasive to those who like to get a bit personal in their communication. A few personal and friendly comments can grease the wheels for results for you.
Specific	You are sure to tell people what you want.	Get precise. Sometimes you are in too big of a hurry to consider the details.
Targeted	You are clear about the results you are targeting. You keep your eyes on the goal, and your words reflect that. You are firm and resolved in your direction—you mean what you say. Clarity and directness are your trademarks.	You can over-focus and miss the big picture. You can underestimate obstacles in your path.
Say What You Mean (Think, Want)	People do not have to guess what your opinion is. They know when you are upset or frustrated and they know what you want. That gives them the comfort of knowing there will not be unforeseen time bombs.	Be collaborative. While you are excellent at informing others of what you think and feel, you are likely to be less open to the thoughts and feelings of others.

PowerPhrase Principle	Achiever Strengths	Achiever Areas For Development
Say What You Mean (Feel)	People know when they have upset you, so there is no worry of stepping on a landmine with you.	Get vulnerable. You often avoid expressing appreciation, sorrow, grief and regret. There are times where getting vulnerable gets results.
Mean What You Say	You have tremendous power of will behind your words.	Avoid being rigid and overly demanding.
Don't Be Mean When You Say It	People have the comfort of knowing where they stand with you.	Get compassionate. You underestimate the needs of others for personal reinforcement. While you are rarely deliberately unkind, you can come across as rude because you are so focused on results that you can seem abrupt. You also tend to order others around and overlook the need to listen.

Achiever PowerPhrase Prescriptions: Below are phrases that you probably don't use enough...and need to.

Short: (Avoid being abrupt)
• No hurry...let's just visit for a while.
• Tell me more.

Specific:
• What I want precisely is...
• The relevant details are...

Focused/targeted:
• The way this fits into the bigger picture is...

Say What You Mean: Think/ Want
- Does this work for you?
- What is your opinion on this?

Say What You Mean: Feelings
- How nice to see you!
- I appreciate the job you did on that.
- I was offended by that remark.
- I'm sorry.

Don't Be Mean When You Say It
- How are you?
- Don't worry about it.
- Is there anything you need from me?

Reflective: Task-Oriented with a Careful Pace

You take your time and focus on the task at hand, information and procedures. You think things through before you take action and you create systems and procedures for everything you do. Your thinking is logical and your words are logical as well. You go from A to B to C to D and it is easy to follow your message. You choice of words is precise, which minimizes confusion.

The table below evaluates the Reflective communication style according to the PowerPhrase principles, and highlights the strengths and areas for development. PowerPhrases are short, specific, focused expressions that say what you mean (think, feel and want), and mean what you say without being mean when you say it.

PowerPhrase Principle	Reflective Strengths	Reflective Areas For Development
Short	You only speak when you have something to say.	Get succinct. You often include too much detail and find it difficult to be brief. You need to abridge your analysis to a brief, understandable review.
Specific	When you say you'll be there at 3:32, you are there at 3:32. Your facts and details are accurate, dependable and reliable.	Get simple. Those who do not have the mind for details that you do cannot follow your level of analysis. You need to distill your words to the most significant details.
Targeted	You can focus to the depth of precision. When you study or describe something you follow it to the final conclusion without distraction or wavering. Your logic in description is impeccable.	Get comprehensive. You are the proverbial "Can't see the forest for the trees" personality. Oh, you see every tree, and want to describe every tree in detail, but need to make mention of the outcome and big picture. You also can be inflexible about alternative views. You also can get obsessive, and have trouble letting go when your world is not in perfect order.

PowerPhrase Principle	Reflective Strengths	Reflective Areas For Development
Say What You Mean (Think)	You consider your thoughts with care before you speak them. When you express your thoughts, they are very carefully formulated.	Your thoughts need to be better balanced with feeling. You are likely to wait until you are certain of your thoughts, which keeps you from the benefit of others' input.
Say What You Mean (Feel)	When you express feelings, you really mean them.	Get personal. Your conversation can sound impersonal and devoid of emotion. People often have to guess what you are feeling. (Of course, you may not know that yourself.)
Mean What You Say	You are so certain of your facts that you can bet your retirement fund on them. (And you are so cautious you probably did not lose your principal when the market tanked.) You do not say anything unless you can speak with absolute precision and certainty. You mean everything you say, and that's a fact.	You can be rigid about what you say because you thought so carefully about it. You need to allow more room for the fallibility of others.
Don't Be Mean When You Say It	Your considered nature keeps you from blurting out hurtful things you regret later.	Your attention to detail can cause you to be critical, rigid and unkind. You are more focused on tasks than people, and as a result, you can come across as hurtful.

Reflective PowerPhrase Prescriptions: Below are phrases that you probably don't use enough ... and need to.

Short:

• I will sum this up briefly.
• Here's the short version.

Specific:
- Here's the essence of what you need to know here.
- It isn't perfect, but it's good enough.
- Let me tell you the most critical details.

Focused/targeted:
- The way this fits into the big picture is...
- This affects us personally by...
- Let's consider the big picture.
- It'll show up.
- I don't think bending that rule will create any problems.
- What this means to you is...

Say What You Mean: Feelings
- It's great to see you!
- That warms my heart.
- I know the news is disappointing. While I can't change the facts, I'm sorry to have such disappointing news.
- I'm excited to tell you...

Say What You Mean: Want
- Here is the action I recommend.
- The conclusion is...
- What I need from you is...

Don't Be Mean When You Say It
- How do you feel about it?
- It's not how we do it now, but let's look at the possibilities.
- I don't expect you to get it perfect.

It Does Take All Kinds to Make a World

The tips and recommendations listed here are not intended to make everyone the same. Celebrate your strengths and consider your weaknesses as areas to develop to round yourself out. And just for fun, try the phrases that are ones you don't often use. See if it works for you, and at the same time, it will allow you to see what it is like to be someone else!

Find your communication style online at:
http://www.speakstrong.com/inventory/

Say what you mean, and
Mean what you say, but–
**Don't be mean when
you say it.**

A PowerPhrase a Week at www.SpeakStrong.com

Free Stickers available at SpeakStrong.com

BIBLIOGRAPHY

Books

Baber, Anne and Lynne Waymon. *Great Connections. Small Talk and Networking for Businesspeople.* Woodbridge, VA: Impact Publications. 1991.

Booher, Dianna. *Communicate With Confidence.* New York: McGraw Hill. 1994.

Booher, Dianna. *The New Secretary.* New York: Facts on File Publications, 1985.

Breitman, Patti, and Connie Hatch. *How to Say No Without Feeling Guilty.* New York: Bantam, 2000.

Caroselli, Marlene Ed.D. *Hiring & Firing.* Mission, KS: SkillPath Publications, 1991.

Caroselli, Marlene Ed.D. *Meetings that Work.* Mission, KS: SkillPath Publications, 1991.

Cohen, Herb. *You Can Negotiate Anything.* Don Mills Ontario: Lyle Stuart Inc, 1980.

Dobson, Michael and Deborah Singer. *Managing Up.* New York: Amacom, 1999.

Donaldson, Michael, and Mimi. *Negotiating for Dummies.* Foster City CA: IDG Books Worldwide, Inc., 1996.

Gamble, Michael & Teri. *Sales Scripts That Sell.* New York: Prentice Hall Publications, 1992.

Griffin, Jack. *How to Say It™ at Work.* Paramus N.J.: Prentice Hall Press, 1998.

Friedman, Paul. How to *Deal With Difficult People.* Mission, KS: SkillPath Publications, 1994.

Larsen, Linda. *True Power.* Sarasota, Florida: Brandywine Publications, 2000.

Levinson, Jay Conrad. *Guerrilla Negotiating.* New York: John Wiley & Sons, 1999.

Mindel, Phyllis. *How to Say It™ for Women.* Paramus, N.J.: Prentice Hall Press, 2001.

Nickerson, Pat. *Managing Multiple Bosses.* New York: Amacom, 1999.

Pollan, M. Stephen and Mark Levine. *Lifescripts.* New York: Macmillan, 1996.

Rackham, Neil. *Spin Selling,* New York: McGraw Hill, 1988.

Schiffman, Stephan. *Cold Calling Techniques (That Really Work!).* Holbrook, MA.: Adams Media Corporation,1990.

Shouse, Deborah. *Breaking the Ice: How to Improve Your On-the-Spot Communications Skills.* Mission, KS.:SkillPath Publications, 1993.

Towers, Mark. *Dynamic Delegation,* Mission, KS: SkillPath Publications, 1993.

Weiss, Donald. *Why Didn't I Say That?!* New York: Amacom, 1994.

Videos

Scofield, Carol. *Conflict Management Skills for Women.* Mission, KS: SkillPath Publications, 1994.

Audios

Covey, Stephen. *The 7 Habits of Highly Effective People.* Provo, Utah: Franklin Covey Co., 1989,1997.

Fine, Debra. *The Fine Art of Small Talk.* Boulder, CO.: Career Track, 1996.

Flemming, Dr. Carol. *The Serious Business of Small Talk.* Mission, KS: SkillPath Publications, 1996.

Larsen, Linda. *12 Secrets to High Self-Esteem.* Mission, KS: SkillPath Publications. 1999.

Speaker's Roundtable. The Pros Speak About Success. Mission, KS: SkillPath Publications, 1999.

Walther, George. *Power Talking Skills.* Boulder, CO.: Career Track™, 1991.

Command Attention in 6 Easy Steps

The Latest Communication Techniques
From a World-Class Coach Who Teaches Top Executives and Powerful People How to Speak Effectively

If you'd like to learn a new language to open up honest dialogue instantly, resolve sensitive situations quickly and effectively, and avoid being taken advantage of, ignored and passed over, then get *How to Use PowerPhrases*.

Here's why. *How to Use PowerPhrases* takes *PowerPhrases!* to the next level of practice. **It's more than principles:** it provides the actual words you need for situations you face every day.

How to Use PowerPhrases includes the same proven communication techniques Meryl Runion teaches when working with IBM, the FBI and the IRS.

Order Today!
www.speakstrong.com

Here's what's in *How to Use PowerPhrases*

- **250 pages packed with powerful phrases.**
  Get the best words for your challenging conversations.

- **Success stories from people who have practiced the PowerPhrase techniques.**
  Learn from the experience of others like you.

- **Answers to questions from Meryl's newsletter subscribers.**
  Read how Meryl recommends handling the most vexing and perplexing problems.

- **5 chapters on dealing with anger and relationship issues.**
  Discover how to use anger as a tool—not a weapon.

- **Techniques to ask for what you want.**
  Be your own advocate.

- **The truth about apologizing.**
  Gain forgiveness and respect for admitting your errors.

- **Ice breakers.**
  Your guide to creating an instant connection with people you want to know.

- **The six secrets of PowerPhrases.**
  Know what is a PowerPhrase and what isn't.

- **PowerPhrase Quiz**
  Determine your "PowerPhrase Potential."

- **The definition of Poison Phrases**
  Learn the words to avoid at all costs.

Don't take my word for it. Listen to what readers say.

"Your book has saved my professional and personal self-confidence with communicating. My conversations and correspondence were long, drawn out, and the other person would get lost in "words." My tendencies were to get the "last word" in a conversation, sometimes with a little barb, thinking I was leaving a lasting impression. Wrong…. Thank you for your saying 'say what you mean, mean what you say, without being mean when you say it.' That one phrase sums it up!" **Kim Hawks**

"This book helped me to learn how to communicate effectively while continuing to be a really nice person that gives and gets respect." A Reader

"It's immediately practical and useful. I learned how to respond to my critical boss, assertively address a backstabber, and most importantly, convey my anger and disappointment without blaming the other person. That lesson alone was worth way more than the price of the book. What a value! I'm using what I learned in this book every day." **Cindi Myers**

"I have tried the "Power Phrases" and they work!" Mary Glenn

Act now

Use the order form in the back of this book or order at *www.speakstrong.com*
For more information, tips and to order, go to *www.speakstrong.com/howtouse.html*

"I could not believe how smooth the review process was this year as a result of this book." Laurie Giacomino

Do you *hate* performance reviews?
This guide shows you how they can be satisfying and rewarding.

I f you'd like to know what to say and not to say in performance reviews, to look forward to giving and receiving performance reviews, and to have a seamless system of performance management that culminates in an integrated performance review, then this might be the most important guide in your performance management library.

Here's why: This book is a quick and efficient resource to make performance reviews the positive management tool they were intended to be.

Here is a summary of the benefits this book offers:

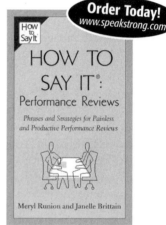

Order Today!
www.speakstrong.com

HOW TO
SAY IT®:
Performance Reviews

Phrases and Strategies for Painless and Productive Performance Reviews

Meryl Runion and Janelle Brittain

- Five steps for mastering every performance review.
  Know how to orchestrate a performance review like a fine symphony.
- Words to choose and words to lose.
  Get the message across without stepping on verbal landmines.
- Common pitfalls and how to steer clear of them.
  See little problems before they become big problems, and avoid them.
- How to master the art of body language and verbal tone.
  Let your "non-verbals" match your "verbals."
- The totally integrated, or "TIPS" system.
  Make your performance reviews a part of a seamless performance management system.
- Real world success stories to emulate (and blunders to avoid.)
  Learn from the successes — and mistakes — of others.
- Compact. *Find what you need FAST! A pocket-size 207 pages.*
- Hundreds of performance review phrases. Find the words that best describe employee performance.

Don't take my word for it. Listen to what our readers say:

A Must for All Managers! — "This book could not have come at a better time. I was dreading the thought of writing my performance reviews until I read this book. It gave me insight into the importance of the process as well as some key phrases to use to make the writing of the review simple. I could not believe how smooth the review process was this year as a result. I wrote my reviews with confidence and it took me half the time it normally takes! I passed it along to my managers and colleagues I was so impressed. Great job, ladies, on making a potentially tired subject alive and refreshing again!" *Laura Giacomino*

Required Reading for Every Supervisor! — "Having recently redeveloped and launched our Performance Management Program, the title of this book really caught my interest. It has been my experience that the best designed Performance Management Program falls short of its intended goal unless it is well communicated to the recipients. Meryl's book offers an extensive selection of phrases and terms for every level of interaction. This book is be a MUST READ for every new supervisor and an excellent CONVERSATION ENHANCER for the seasoned ones. I would highly recommend this be kept in the top drawer of anyone who has the occasion to discuss performance with an employee!" *Lawrence Palmer*

Use the order form in the back of this book or order at *www.speakstrong.com*
Don't wait—for more information, tips and to order, go to
www.speakstrong.com/performancereviews.html

The Number One Secrets of Successful Managers
tells you everything you need to know about managing others

I f you'd like to motivate your employees to do their jobs, reduce stress in the workplace and unleash the power in everyday leadership, get *The Number One Secrets of Successful Managers*.

Here's why: Hal Pitt developed a unique "Number Ones" approach to management that will help you focus on what will get you the best results. In practical, down-to-earth terms, you'll learn key concepts and strategies that have formed the best practices lists of thousands of successful managers.

Revealing Case In Point... stories bring the Number One ideas home with real examples. An Action Plan at the end of each chapter gives you the opportunity to apply the principles and become a Number One success story!

Hal Pitt knows what he's talking about. Known as a highly effective teacher, public speaker, and communicator, Hal E. Pitt has taught seminars on team building, leadership, communication, and management in the United States, Canada, Australia, and the United Kingdom. He managed more than one hundred medical personnel in a stressful emergency room; recruited, trained, and managed instructors in various training programs; and designed and developed training sessions and model medical programs and curricula. Hal Pitt understands group dynamics and is creative in developing material that is both powerful and entertaining.

The chapter titles say it all.

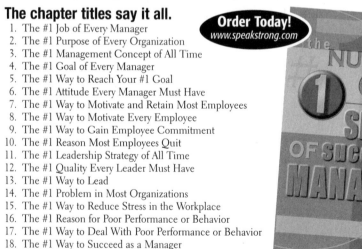

Order Today!
www.speakstrong.com

1. The #1 Job of Every Manager
2. The #1 Purpose of Every Organization
3. The #1 Management Concept of All Time
4. The #1 Goal of Every Manager
5. The #1 Way to Reach Your #1 Goal
6. The #1 Attitude Every Manager Must Have
7. The #1 Way to Motivate and Retain Most Employees
8. The #1 Way to Motivate Every Employee
9. The #1 Way to Gain Employee Commitment
10. The #1 Reason Most Employees Quit
11. The #1 Leadership Strategy of All Time
12. The #1 Quality Every Leader Must Have
13. The #1 Way to Lead
14. The #1 Problem in Most Organizations
15. The #1 Way to Reduce Stress in the Workplace
16. The #1 Reason for Poor Performance or Behavior
17. The #1 Way to Deal With Poor Performance or Behavior
18. The #1 Way to Succeed as a Manager
19. The #1 Reason for Wanting to Be a Manager
20. The Number Ones Revisited

Act now

Use the order form in the back of this book or order at *www.speakstrong.com*
For more information, tips and to order, go to *www.speakstrong.com/secrets.html*

NEW – LIVE PRESENTATIONS ON DVD

Next! And Other Empowered Ways to Deal With Rejection
A thriver's tool box for success

"Last year I received a call asking if I would present a session at a conference on the topic of rejection. Apparently the organizer thought I must be some kind of expert on the topic — and she was right. I remember driving home from the airport so late one Friday night that it was really Saturday AM exhausted and discouraged. It had been a week of painful setbacks. Was it time to throw in the towel, I wondered? But then I realized that what I was doing took courage. I was continuing on in the face of rejection. It was then that I latched on to my personal slogan —  DARE TO BE ORDINARY! Because the learning curve to being extraordinary can take you through some very ordinary places — filled with self-doubt and rejection. If you ever get discouraged by rejection, this DVD is for you." **Meryl Runion**

This DVD is a live presentation with added handouts from the author of **PowerPhrases**. It provides stories you will relate to, exercises you will benefit from and specific action steps to help you turn rejection into a tool for success rather than an obstacle.

Meryl is her usual, lighthearted and good-natured self in this dynamic, practical and useful presentation.

The Difference Between Lightning Bugs and Lightning Bolts:
How to Use PowerPhrases to Say What You Mean, Mean What You Say and Get What You Want

A one-hour live presentation on DVD from the creator of *PowerPhrases!* Mark Twain says that the difference between the perfect words and the almost perfect words is like the difference between lightning bugs and lightning bolts.

This entertaining one-hour keynote tells you how to turn your words into lightning bolts of communication that say what you mean and mean what you say and get you what you want.

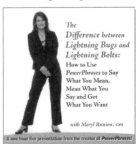

- Learn the eight lame excuses that you use to avoid speaking up.
- Discover what the riskiest conversations are.
- Understand how the three brains operate and how that affects word choice.
- Hear about the six secrets of PowerPhrases in action.
- Discover a simple formula to capture what you want to say.
- Watch a live presentation of The Legend of Mighty Mouth… And so much more.

Use the order form in the back of this book or order at *www.speakstrong.com*

311

If you prefer to listen, this audio is for you.

PowerPhrases® Amplified:
Say What You Mean,
Mean What You Say, Get What You Want

"If you're auditory, like me, *you'll want the unabridged version of* **How to Use PowerPhrases** *on CD. I like to listen to knowledge as I drive around in my car, chop my vegetables, clean my house and do other activities. I find that information that I listen to stays with me longer. Many people have told me they listen to* **PowerPhrases® Amplified** *over and over again."* **Meryl Runion**

The unabridged audio CD versions of *How to Use PowerPhrases,* **PowerPhrases® Amplified** provides in-depth understanding of the secrets that make PowerPhrases effective, and it provides countless stories and illustrations of how PowerPhrases work in action. You will walk away with practical and priceless solutions you can use right now.

Discover how to:
- Avoid "Poison Phrases" that are ineffective or backfire
- Perfect the connection – quickly when seconds count
- Disagree without being disagreeable yourself
- Apologize sincerely without groveling
- Get others to speak freely and openly
- Say no with grace, tact, and resolve
- Make your opinion matter most
- Ask so you will receive

Six information-packed audio CD's and a workbook on CD.
You'll WANT to listen again and again, until you'll find yourself practicing skills you didn't know you had.

Order today with the form at the back of the book, or visit
www.speakstrong.com/amplified.html

You are invited to a light-hearted and entertaining experience
of communication transformation in Colorado Springs
Come to the next retreat of

Some Boats Need to Be Rocked: How to
Use PowerPhrases to Talk About What Really Matters.
YOU'LL *LOVE* HOW IT ROCKS YOUR WORLD

If you'd like to speak up, be heard and be understood, discover your communication style, learn how to talk to people with different styles from your own and learn a new language to open up honest dialogue instantly, then call today to register for the next retreat, *Some Boats Need to Be Rocked.*

Here's why:

People who speak up and do it well are happier, more successful and enjoy life more. This retreat teaches you which boats need to be rocked, how to rock them and how not to rock them.

Here's the best part:

This is not about what works for anyone else, **this is all about YOU.**

Read what former participants have said:

"A life changing experience. I am glad I waited to write you to realize the enormous impact the retreat had on me. Thanks. Last week Debbie asked me who I was and what did I do with her Ivan? She said it was like I had a lobotomy or something down there. I'm working on some success stories too." *Ivan Haag*

"**The days flew by.** The worst thing about this seminar is that it had to end." *Heidi Roberts*

"**Each person was given the luxury** of being able to ask questions about specific problems/scenarios and receive an individual response. It was also a fun, non threatening, safe environment to discuss very personnel issues." *Caro Cook*

"We were not only able to learn about the subject but also a significant amount about ourselves. This feature alone would make this workshop stand **head and shoulders above any other.**" *Mark Parameter*

For more information, email: *MerylRunion@speakstrong.com*
For more information, visit *www.speakstrong/springsretreat.html*

ADDITIONAL RESOURCES

Item	Quantity	Price	Total
Books:			
Power Phrases!® Newly revised with multi-media CD	_____	$ 29.00	_____.__
How to Use Power Phrases Find the words for every situation	_____	$ 12.00	_____.__
Perfect Phrases for Managers *& Supervisors*	_____	$ 9.00	_____.__
How To Say It: Performance Reviews by Meryl Runion and Janelle Brittain	_____	$ 9.95	_____.__
Number One Secrets *of Successful Managers* by Hal Pitt	_____	$ 20.00	_____.__
Audio/Video:			
Power Phrases Amplified 6 CDs and a workbook	_____	$ 65.00	_____.__
Lightning Bugs and Lightening Bolts DVD	_____	$ 19.95	_____.__
Next!—Ways to Deal with Rejection DVD	_____	$ 19.95	_____.__

Shipping: Overseas orders? Contact *MerylRunion@speakstrong.com* for rates.

Add $3.75 for your first item			$ 3.75
$2.00 for each additional item	_____	× $2.00	_____.__
Sales Tax Colorado Residents add 2.9%			_____.__

Total:

*Mail form with payment or
credit card number to:*

**SpeakStrong
4265 Outpost Road
Cascade CO 80809**

Order online at *www.speakstrong.com*

Ship to:

Name:_____

Address: _____

City/State: _____

Zip:_____ Phone:____ - ____ - ____

Clients Include...

 Internal Revenue Service
DEPARTMENT OF THE TREASURY

 LOCKHEED MARTIN

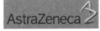 NOVARTIS

 U.S. Cellular

 Current®
Where Staying In Touch Is Affordable & Fun

 PROGRESSIVE

 AstraZeneca

 Travelers™

The Genuine. The Original.
 OVERHEAD DOOR®

 ANHEUSER BUSCH
Companies

ADVENTIS

Johnson & Johnson

 ERICSSON

 Jenkens & Gilchrist

 UNITED STATES ENVIRONMENTAL PROTECTION AGENCY

 The Patent Office
PATENTS • DESIGNS • COPYRIGHT • TRADE MARKS

 Department of Veterans Affairs

 BELLSOUTH®

 GE  General Electric Company

 LEER

 IBM®

 Honeywell

 CardinalHealth

 ARIZONA

 MOUNT HOLYOKE

Global  Security.org

 ABWA
AMERICAN BUSINESS WOMEN'S ASSOCIATION

 SIEMON NETWORK CABLING SOLUTIONS United States

 Bairnsdale
Regional Health Service

 KING/DREW MEDICAL CENTER

 WV WOMEN'S VISION® FOUNDATION
The Voice for Corporate Women

 ARCTEC Services

 MARSH

 Hydromat® Inc.
precision transfer machines

 Elementary Secondary Middle Continuing
New York State EDUCATION

 Joyce Meyer Ministries

 QUEST

Ohio Department of HEALTH

Speak as if every
word matters.
It does.

A PowerPhrase a Week

Home I Articles I Hire Meryl I SpeakStrong Store I Free Stuff I Teleseminars I Blog I Contact

**Issue 313
June 19, 2008**

This Week in the World

PowerPhrase of the Week

Poison Phrase of the Week

Ask Meryl

Reader Success Story

Reader Comments

READ MERYL'S BLOG

www.speakstrong.com

A PowerPhrase a Week
Archives

If you are receiving this in error, please scroll down for information about safe email removal.

This Week in the World
The power of tears, anger and getting out of your head

My recent article _Constructive Anger: How to SpeakStrong when you're seeing red_ received hundreds of hits and scores of forwards. Last week's _The Secret Power of Tears_ has broken all records for popular articles.

If your emotions or someone else's ever feel like the tornado the cub scouts faced in Iowa last week, read these articles and pass them on.

If you stifle emotions instead of manage them you'll shut down your passion, and with it, your strength and power.

You know you're
intellectualizing when...

Many people respond intellectually to situations where an emotional response would be more appropriate. (The opposite is also true, of course.) I'd like your help with my latest list: You know you're intellectualizing when...

1. You know you're intellectualizing when someone writes you a love poem and you point out a misplaced comma.

2. You know you're intellectualizing when you explain why the rainbow is so colorful and forget to admire its beauty.

3. You know you're intellectualizing when you tell a woman in childbirth "your labor pains are interesting sensations worthy

Sample Newsletter   Sign up for A PowerPhrase a Week at **www.speakstrong.com**

www.speakstrong.com/ecourse.html